RED

RED

Life Lessons from a Father

Harold "Red" Allen
As Told To
Darius Allen

Varsity Club

PUBLISHED BY VARSITY CLUB PUBLISHING
a division of Varsity Club Enterprises, LLC.

www.varsityclubinc.com

Varsity Club

is a registered trademark of Varsity Club Enterprises, LLC.
Manufactured and printed in the United States of America
Library of Congress Cataloging in Publication Data

Red: Life Lessons from a Father/Harold "Red" Allen with
Darius Allen
1. Life Lessons 2. Fatherhood. 3. Philosophies

Library of Congress Control Number: 2014933425

ISBN: 978-0-9916190-0-9

THIS BOOK IS DEDICATED
TO MY MOTHER,
RUTH MCKNIGHT.

Contents

A Father's Words

Acknowledgments

With gratitude, I want to thank my best friend and youngest son, Darius, for organizing my ideas and words into book form. I would also like to thank him for his guidance and patience, for this was a great father and son adventure.

To the rest of the family, my lovely wife Gwendolyn, Harold Jr., Marcus, Damon, Michael and Michelle, I could not have accomplished this goal of writing my life lessons without your support and everlasting love.

Introduction

I come to you as a man who has had the privilege to be called a father, a title that I earned and one that I carry with honor. The weight of being a father is still heavy, and the wear and tear on my body from handling my responsibilities is clearly visible. Fatherhood speeds up the aging process. Grey hairs appear overnight. But at my young age of 79, I can proudly declare that there are few honors greater than being called a father.

This book is a list of my life lessons that I've learned to live by. Life's challenges that I was confronted with in my childhood and that continue to humble me in my adulthood. I've seen and experienced a lot during my travels and without a doubt, I can tell you that the years may change, but the principles of life don't. That's the truth. I can only give it to you like I know how. I'm too old to change up now. Although, I like to believe I'm only 39 years old and holding.

RED

We All Have A Beginning

Always Think Big

They say, "Everything is bigger in Texas," well, they must have forgotten about my birthplace. We have no control in determining where and when we begin our journey. But one thing is for sure, we all have a beginning. Where we begin our journey shouldn't make or break us, but it will shape us. My journey began on June 17, 1934. I, Harold Eugene Allen, was born in a humble, gabled roof house, on Washington Street in Denison, Texas.

Denison is a small town where in 1934 there were 13,850 residents and even today, the population has never exceeded 30,000. That's nothing compared to the hundreds of thousands of Texans that were living in Dallas and Austin in the 1930s. Located in North Texas, Denison is a railroad town, the last stop leaving Texas as you enter "The Sooner State", Oklahoma.

The founders of Denison were on the right track when they announced their piece of land as the "Gate City of Texas". Once the owners of the MKT Railroad, which stood for Missouri-Kansas-Texas, decided to create a railway across Indian Territory and right through Denison, this small town went from a new frontier to a buzzing central station for shipping goods and freight. One of those items was ice and with Denison having the first Ice Factory in North Texas, The Crystal Ice Co., business was booming. In addition, a livestock broker named Joseph G. McCoy, sparked economic growth by establishing the Atlantic & Texas Refrigerating Co., which made refrigerated beef shipments throughout Texas.

Denison took that economic success and invested it right back into its people. Education became a top priority and we led the way when we opened up the first free, public school in the entire state of Texas. And with big town ambition, we also emerged as a large center for job opportunities. Texans from neighboring towns and Sooners from Oklahoma traveled to work at the MKT Railroad, the Perrin Air Force Base, the Peanut Factory and the Levi Strauss plant.

Our history is not only attached to the expansion of the railroad, and just like any big town, we had our share of good luck and happenstance. The first ice cream soda was an accidental creation by Denison ice cream maker, Joseph Anton Euper. While others dispute that claim, you know he definitely gets my vote. On the other hand, I'm still debating on how I feel about "Doc" Holliday, who is widely known for being one of the deadliest gunslingers in the West. Years before his relationship with Wyatt Earp and the Gunfight at the O.K. Corral, "Doc" opened up an office and practiced dentistry in Denison until fleeing the state on a trail of illegal gambling charges.

Now, if there is one thing that most people do know about my hometown, is that it's the birthplace of the 34th President of the United States, Dwight D. Eisenhower. That's Denison's claim to fame.

Let me also remind everyone that in 2009, Captain Chesley B. "Sully" Sullenberger successfully landed US Airways Flight 1549 into the Hudson River after the engine was struck by a flock of geese minutes after takeoff. The "Miracle On The Hudson", was no small act of heroism. All passengers and crew were evacuated safely. This American hero was born in Denison.

Lastly, for all you football fans, it's also the birthplace of Hall of Fame cornerback, Michael Haynes. He always came up big for the New England Patriots and then later in his career for the Los Angeles Raiders.

So don't tell Denisonians that Denison's a small town. Thinking beyond our boundaries and dreaming the impossible dream is what we do. No matter if you come from humble beginnings or you're facing challenges that weigh heavy on your shoulders, never believe you're destined to do small things.

If you're from a small town, think big. If you're from a big town, think even bigger.

A Leopard Can't Change Its Spots

Just like a leopard, there are spots that we are born with that we can't change. I'm proud to be from Denison, but I didn't ask to be born there. I surely didn't ask to come into the world during a time of segregation and the Great Depression. I simply had to live with those spots.

There is one particular spot that has the most significance, and how we deal with this spot can affect our entire lives. We must all come to peace with the realization that we do not choose our parents. We have no control of the conditions that we are born into, but this doesn't mean we are completely powerless. We will eventually reach an age, where we will have control over how we choose to view our circumstances and the people in them. When I reached that pivotal age to make my decision, I chose to make the best of my situation and to appreciate the spots that I was given.

My father's name was Mildred Bernard Allen. To this day, I still wonder how his parents came up with his first name. He was a handsome man with wavy hair and a short mustache. My mother's name was Ruth McKnight, a petite woman with a smile as big as Texas. My parents were in high school when I was born, and marriage was not part of their adolescent plans. As soon as I entered the world, they went their separate ways.

When I was 2 years old, my mother Ruth married a man named Jodie Clark. In time, my father married a woman named Erma. I was an only child, but as the years passed I became the eldest of 12 kids. I have six 6 brothers and 6 sisters.

I would love to tell stories of how I wanted to follow in my father's footsteps. How each day as he prepared for work, I would mimic his every move and pretend I was a man getting ready to bravely face the world. That was not the case. The reality is I didn't spend too much time with my father growing up. When I was 7 years old, I lived with him and his wife for three months, in Vernon, Texas. That was it. Three months that flew by so quickly, I barely remember unpacking the little bit of clothing I had.

That limited time consisted of me peeking at the newly dealt cards that Erma and my father held while they played bid whist, a popular card game at the time. My other activity was making long walks to a nightclub to interrupt my father's poker games.

Just about every evening while Erma was preparing dinner, I was given the word to go across town to pick up my father. The nightclub was so crowded that patrons didn't even notice a wide-eyed youngster maneuvering his way through the crowd towards a smoked filled backroom where the pool hustlers and card sharks held court. I would walk up curiously to the table, and my father would give me a reluctant nod—he knew it was time to go. We would begin our walk back home, rarely exchanging words of wisdom, and nothing more than a few glances. I guess our thoughts were always on Erma's home cooking, but I know that's just a convenient excuse to mask our lack of a connection.

I was never given an explanation for his reserved nature. I wish I could recite some stories about his life, better yet, his childhood. *I don't think my expectations were too high.* I would have gladly settled for a story about the dangers of playing poker. In those three months, I was only left with my interpretation of how my father felt about me. Although, I never heard my father utter the words, "I love you", as we walked, and occasionally looked at each other, I got the feeling that he did. It was just expressed in his own unique way.

Unfortunately, what I do remember most about my stay in Vernon was being picked on by the Johnson brothers who lived next door. I was the new face in the neighborhood and they didn't take a liking to my light complexion. They classified my skin color as "light, bright and damn near white." And to top it off, I had a sandy reddish hair color so I was an easy target for this family of bullies.

In their eyes, I was not "black" enough and they tried their best to let me know verbally and physically. Every day, they felt a need to remind me of certain spots that I was given. Spots that I could not change. Spots that I inherited when I was born. I strongly felt that I looked like my mother and that was all right with me. So every day, as the Johnson boys poked fun at me, I became more and more comfortable with my spots. My skin got thicker. I quickly learned to love my spots. I didn't let their vision and thoughts of me affect me at all. It's funny —years later those particular spots would be the source of my nickname.

Those are my lasting memories of Vernon, Texas.

Living with my mother in Denison was a different story. Where my father was reserved and stoic, my mother and I talked openly and expressed our emotions freely. No topic was off limits. We often borrowed our topics from her favorite radio soap opera shows, Stella Dallas and Our Gal Sunday. I sat quietly alongside my mother listening to the rags to riches story lines that kept us glued to the radio. Those episodes touched on dramatic themes like revenge, backstabbing, and infidelity, issues that I couldn't fully comprehend at a young age. The cowboy adventures of Tom Mix were more my style and speed, but the time spent bonding with her was worth all of the head-scratching.

My mother worked hard a domestic worker, doing laundry, ironing clothes and cleaning houses. She worked hard every day, and her only break was when we woke up early on Sunday mornings to walk to Hopewell Baptist Church for service. She made sure I was an active member. She schooled me on the importance of having faith in God and trusting his word. Just like any kid, I had a couple of questions to ask God. *What do you really look like? What plans do you have for me?* Whenever I asked my mother these same questions, she told me to, "Keep living and sooner or later you'll feel a hand on your shoulder guiding you." At the same time, I was told not to wait for anything to drop out of the sky. She believed that God helps those who help themselves.

She always spoke to me as an adult. Being pampered and coddled were never options for me in her book. Even when I did hear the words, "I love you", they weren't delivered with the softness of a hug. I was given a heavy dose of what many from her generation would call "tough love". She looked me in the eyes and told me, "You gonna have good days and bad days. The key is to live with both." I think she understood early that sheltering me from my small town and the outside world would be a mistake. I was allowed the freedom to roam and play outside until the sunset. I had her trust, but if I crossed the line, she let me have it. In her simple way of rearing, she taught me that certain acts have consequences. She was left handed, and I was always a sucker for her right hand when it came to being disciplined.

When it came to my stepfather, he never disciplined me. I wouldn't allow it. We didn't see eye-to-eye and we exchanged few words. Whenever we shared eye contact, our glares reminded each other that we weren't blood related. His actions made it difficult for me to look past that fact. He always spoke in a harsh tone that carried resentment, a bitterness that didn't stem from within the house. I witnessed him come home on payday, quickly leave and then return drunk with no money in his pocket. Whatever hint of a relationship that was present was broken when I overheard him yell in an argument with my mother, "He's not *my kid*, so I don't have to take care of him." Once I heard that, the line was drawn and I stayed on my side.

Although my mother was aware of the tension that seemed to grow by the day, there was never a time where I thought that she wasn't in my corner. My mother didn't jump in the middle and try to mend our relationship. She just let it be.

The years passed and my family life on Washington Street continued to be rocky. On occasion I would receive updates on my father's whereabouts. Once my mother told me that he moved to Tucson, Arizona to work for the Greyhound bus station. Somedays, I was told there were sightings of my father in Denison. I welcomed the tidbits of information, but I was never excited. I always felt it would have been better if he paid me a visit—that day never happened. My father passed away in 1946 when I was 12 years old. Even the news about his death was given with little detail. However, I was finally able to compile a solid story. Supposedly, he was in Denison recovering from surgery and he caught pneumonia while being transported from the hospital to his home. His funeral was at Hopewell Baptist Church and I remember standing quietly and emotionless through the whole ceremony. I couldn't describe the feeling I had inside. There was emptiness, but I wasn't consumed with sadness and struggling with anger. I was just still.

After the funeral, I started to reflect on my relationship with my mother. I thought about the experiences with my father and stepfather. I looked at my surroundings. These were spots that I've been given. I couldn't change them, but I did have power to control my attitude towards them and I had power over my actions.

My childhood taught me that I didn't want to be absent in someone's life like my father was in mine. I certainly didn't want to harbor the same bitterness about my circumstances that I encountered with my stepfather. I wanted to move forward. I chose to *forgive but not forget.*

Right then and there, I closed my eyes and quietly made a promise to myself—I took a personal vow that if I ever got married and became a father, I was going to be the best father I could be.

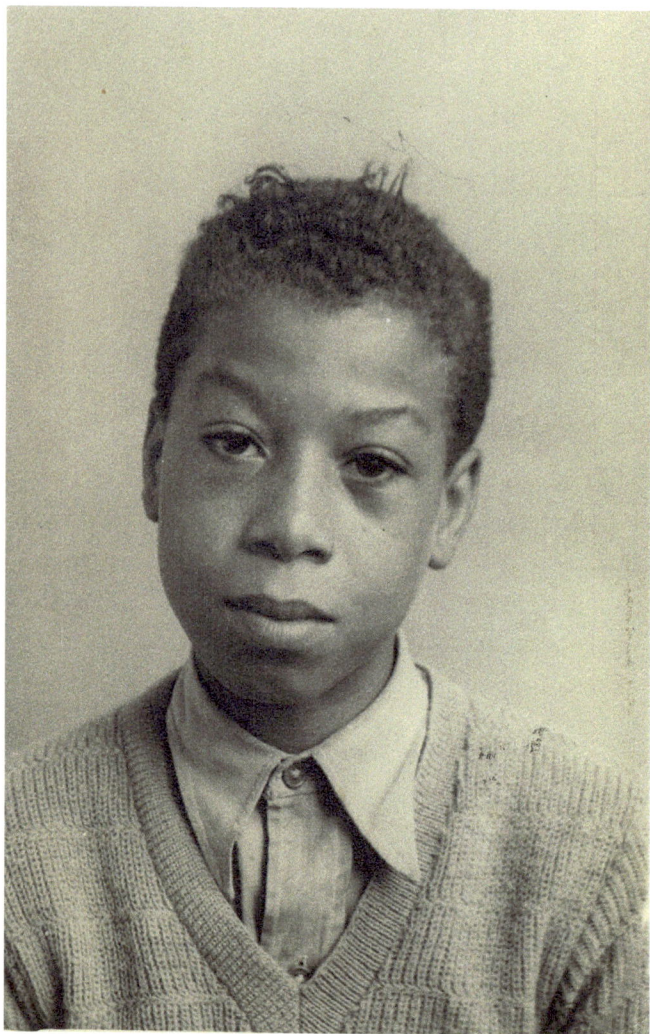

Harold Eugene Allen
Denison, Texas. (1946)

Work With What You Got

One of the most valuable lessons I've learned from my birthplace is to appreciate what you have and not dwell on what you don't have. Growing up in Denison, I never heard anyone use the words "luxury goods". The town was small, the people were simple and you worked with what you got. Believe me, that wasn't much. However, we were too busy having fun to notice.

Once I left the porch, I was involved in a little of everything. Directly across from my mother's house, lived the Golston brothers: Alvin, Billy Ray, Lloyd and Bennie. Billy Ray and I were the same age, so he naturally became my running mate. We wore Levi's jeans with marbles spilling out of the pockets. Alongside the house, we would shoot marbles until the sun went down. Or you may have caught us in the woods running around the creeks with cap pistols playing Cowboys and Indians.

Billy Ray and I became household names in the neighborhood by making grocery store runs for families that didn't want to make the long walk. We were paid in quarters. We'd split the change and more often than not, buy 10-cent comic books. Billy Ray had a thing for Superman. Whereas, I wasn't intrigued by superheroes from distant planets. I had a thing for Red Ryder, the famous fighting cowboy.

Sometimes when we had a fist full of quarters, we headed to Lemons Café, which was 4 blocks from my house. It was a popular hangout for the high school kids who wanted to socialize, but we only went for one thing: the chili. Each bite was a chunk of ground beef, juicy red beans and a chili sauce so good that I know the recipe had to be locked away in a safe. I ate so much chili that a schoolmate named Clarence English gave me my first nickname, "Chili Bowl".

Our main hangout was the Red River, the famous river that separates Texas from Oklahoma. At that time, we didn't have a rod and a reel—we had to be innovative. So with a little ingenuity, a branch from a tree, a fishing line and some careful handwork would produce a world-class fishing pole. With our wooden poles, a bucket, a metal fish stringer and .22 rifles in hand, we would walk 6 miles from Washington Street to the Red River.

Billy Ray got his rifle from his father, and I got mine from my Cousin Marie, who would join us on our fishing trips with her husband. She enjoyed fishing, and unlike us, she had a shiny fishing rod and reel that sparkled when it reflected off the sun. It was nice, but I've never known a fish to bite because of the shininess of your rod. Billy Ray and I were quite aware of that. We centered our attention on the fish. It took us a while, but we eventually developed a winning strategy that we kept top secret. With left over change, we bought a small strip of bacon. We used bacon as bait to catch crawfish, and then we used the crawfish as bait to catch the fish. We were masters and the bacon worked like a charm. As soon as it hit the water, the crawfish started clawing. Before they could devour the bacon, we quickly snatched them out of the water. In no time, our little bucket was filled to the top in squirming crawfish.

When it came to catching fish, we only had one competitor. Snakes! Not ordinary snakes, we're talking water moccasins. They were also on the hunt. They kept us on our toes and that's where the rifles came in handy. Whether swimming or slithering through the ground, water moccasins didn't play fair, so we always had to be on alert. We wanted the fish to bite, not the water moccasins.

Denison didn't have a State Fair like Dallas. There was no Ferris wheel line to stand in. No pig race to enjoy. For us, the small town and the Red River provided all the thrills and anxieties of an amusement park. We didn't complain. In fact, we didn't miss a beat. We learned to be resourceful. We had a surplus of imagination and creativity. That's all you need.

At that age, I wasn't familiar with the saying, "Don't try to keep up with the Joneses." If I was, I would have asked the Joneses if they could keep up with us. Always be appreciative of the things you have and the things that money can't buy. Don't get caught up following the lifestyles of others. First of all, you don't even know what they've done to obtain that lifestyle and acquire the things that they have in it. A lot of Joneses are smiling on the outside while crying on the inside. Focus on your happiness and the way to do that is to value what you have, and work with what you got.

Look, Listen And Learn

With the passing of my father and the non-existent relationship I had with my stepfather, the most dominant voice in my life was my mother's. Although I had an open ear and a warm heart for her words and teachings, I always knew there were just some things I needed to hear from a man's perspective. And there were some things I needed to see to believe. I was growing up fast and manhood was around the corner. It had never crossed my mind that I was in need of a father figure. I was quite content with living life and following my inner voice. However, at 13 years old, I knew I didn't have all the answers. I was open to listening and observing those who have *been there and done that*. There is a reason why we're given two eyes, two ears and only one mouth. We're supposed to do much more listening and observing than talking. In my good fortune, I learned that bit of wisdom from an unexpected source: the baseball diamond.

With all the attention Texans give to football, it's easy to forget the rich history of baseball that lives in the state. In the 30s and 40s, minor league baseball flourished throughout the big cities. The whites had the Texas League that consisted of teams in Austin, Fort Worth, Galveston, Dallas, San

Antonio and Houston. And blacks organized teams that barnstormed in those same areas under economic conditions that made it difficult for them to carry the Negro League banner.

In Denison, there was one team that dominated the headlines and that was the all white Sherman-Denison Twins. Luckily, we didn't let that deter our love for America's pastime. On my side of town, semi-pro baseball was the happening pick-up game. The definition of semi-pro may be different today, but back then, it was a league where the working folk played without pay. Maybe that's the reason a youthful 13-year old was able to walk onto the field and get behind the plate.

I played catcher on a semi-pro baseball team with guys that were between 25-40 years old. I was the only kid good enough to play and who was also smart enough to know when to talk and when to keep my mouth shut. I had soft hands, quick feet and a rifle for an arm. I still remember like it was yesterday. Some of the players told me that I resembled another catcher that they played with at Terrell High. I smiled and took it as a compliment, but when they told me that player was my father, Mildred Allen—I got butterflies inside. For the very first time, I felt we shared a common bond. *What a coincidence, we were both catchers.*

Despite being the starting catcher, the team reminded me that I was a kid and I had to know my place. I wasn't shown any favoritism for being

Mildred's son. In the heat of that unforgettable summer, these guys played hard and they played by a set of rules that I quickly had to learn. Little did I know, these rules would become invaluable lessons for a young man on his way to manhood. I might have been wearing a baggy baseball uniform, but make no mistake, I was a student and school was in session.

Do Onto Others, As You Wish They Do Onto You

I learned that when you're dealing with men, you should "Do onto others, as you wish they do onto you." It's all about having good sportsmanship. You either treat a man with respect or disrespect. Those two words govern all men. These men wanted to win, but more importantly baseball provided them with an escape from the harsh realities of segregation and a job market with little opportunity. For those who had hopes for making it to the big leagues with Jackie Robinson, they found the first bus out of Denison. The others played so they could get out of the house. Baseball was a breath of fresh air.

That doesn't mean the competition wasn't intense. There were plenty of fastballs thrown high and tight. The slides into second base came in with spikes high. Everyone was aggressively swinging for the fence. But overall, the level of competition couldn't compare to the level of respect the players shared with each other on the baseball diamond. I was part of a brotherhood and respect was the common thread stitched in all of our uniforms. So showing up another player or an umpire in a disrespectful manner was not only frowned upon, it came with a butt whooping. Being a showboat was not tolerated. The guys simply didn't have time for it. That's not why they played the game.

It's Not Just A Game

At 13, I understood for the first time, that sports were more than just a playful activity. These men loved the game of baseball. They loved what the game stood for. On the field, merit and skill prevailed. Not the color of your skin. It didn't matter your size, height, weight, shape, or if you were pigeon toed or bowlegged. If you could play baseball, that's all that mattered.

A Person That Constantly Uses Profanity Has A Small Vocabulary

I was given a rule that I couldn't use any profanity at all while playing in the field or in the dugout. I remember being taken to the side and specifically being told that a person that constantly uses profanity has a small vocabulary. I quickly learned this rule did not apply to the entire team—it was only for me. I got a chuckle when I would hear my teammates swearing up a storm, however if I uttered any such word, my butt would be planted firmly on the bench. So I obeyed the rule and played it straight. I figured there were millions of words in the dictionary. I might as well use them. I didn't want anything to get in the way of my playing time; and as a result, I also learned I didn't want to have a small vocabulary.

Always Profit By Others' Mistakes

Baseball provided my teammates with a temporary escape from their problems, but that didn't mean I didn't hear about their problems. The baseball diamond was also a sacred place where black men could voice their opinion free of judgment and consequence. As soon as the players started tossing the ball around, the real chatter began. Jokes were told, insults were thrown, dirty laundry was aired out and stress was relieved.

In all this playful banter and backchat, I heard every story in the book. The rookies consulted with the veterans on issues well beyond baseball. The topics varied—from what to do with a two-timing girlfriend that decided to return home—to the correct ways to deal with a friend that owed you money. There was always plenty advice on how to attract the ladies—everyone had two cents to give on that subject. Confrontations with bosses, arguments with the wife, and tales about the first blacks to settle in Denison were all topics tossed around like a baseball.

I listened to every word, catching the gist of every story. The lesson I learned was to try to profit from others' mistakes. I understood that I didn't have to learn everything from experience. I just had to look, listen and learn. Some things in life just weren't for me. And there were some moves I just didn't need to make. *Why suffer the consequences of certain actions, when you already know the outcome? Why test the waters when you already know it's a temperature that you can't handle?* There's no need. The smart person will profit by listening and being observant, picking up what to do and what not to do.

If You're Going to Follow, Follow The Right Example

Speaking of being observant, the biggest impression that was left on me was from the interaction between my teammates and their kids. I witnessed my teammates transition from being ballplayers to fathers. I was able to observe the father-son relationship that I never had. I was also introduced to the father-daughter relationship that I had never seen. Fathers were connecting with their kids. These fathers were enthusiastic, engaged and passionate when they spoke. Their smiles were infectious. Their words were respected. They let everyone know that their relationship with their kids was a priority. That hit me harder than any fastball that blazed into my catcher's mitt. I was shown definitive examples of fathers in action. And these fathers didn't just rear their own kids. I was treated like an extended member of the family. If there was anything I needed, a helping hand was there. If I needed a word of advice, wisdom was shared. If I needed a place to lay my head, the door was opened.

I thought to myself, "That's the type of father I want to be. I want my kids to have those same smiles." I wanted to follow that example.

Get Your Uniform Dirty

Like the majority of young black kids growing up in Denison, I couldn't wait to wear the school colors of maroon and white for the Terrell High Dragons. Terrell High was the only all black high school in Denison, so it was only a matter of time I would get my chance to walk through those hallways.

It is no surprise, that in the state of Texas, when it comes to high school athletics, everything starts and ends with football. I first witnessed the popularity when I watched Billy Ray's oldest brother, Bennie, play for the Dragons. Every Friday night, blacks and whites jam-packed the house—for those 4 quarters of hard-nosed football, the only thing that was considered segregated was the opposing team's sidelines.

When it came time for me to suit up and hit the field, I was more than ready to start the football season. As a sophomore I earned a spot in the secondary as a defensive back. Billy Ray, with his quick feet, was the starting running back. Weeks before the first game, the head coach presented me with a daunting challenge. The interior of the offensive line was having issues in practice protecting the quarterback. We were also having problems with the center-quarterback exchange. If you know anything about football, no time for the quarterback equals zero points on the scoreboard.

The head coach said he talked to several players in private about making a switch to center. We didn't have the biggest roster and most guys were already utility players, filling positions on offense and defense. But no one wanted to be the center. I mean no one, not even the benchwarmers on the team. *I guess some would rather stand on the sideline and look cute in a clean uniform.* My teammates conveniently forgot how important that position was to the offense. It didn't help that the center position was about as popular as being the kicker on the team. There's no bragging rights and glamour being lost in the bottom of a pile. That position rarely gets your name in the headlines. Delivering a big hit or catching a touchdown pass made you the talk of the town, but snapping the ball and blocking huge nose tackles only made you extremely sore and worn out.

When the coach asked me to play center, I was shocked. Evidently my toughness made a strong impression, but playing defensive back and center was a whole new ball game. I wasn't the biggest guy on the team. I only stood 5'9" and weighed around 155 pounds, and that was on a good day. I didn't think I was mentally and physically ready to be in the trenches battling guys twice my size. I started thinking about all the ice packs I would need after every game. I also started to think about a saying that I heard from of an old baseball teammate. He used to say, "Dynamite comes in small packages." I always took a personal liking to that saying.

I knew someone had to do it, so I agreed to take on that challenge. Win or lose, I wanted to help my team.

Looking back, I'm glad the coach asked me to fill that position. Along with being in on every play and never leaving the field with a clean uniform, playing center made me mentally tougher. With every snap, I found grit that I never knew I had inside. Every time I picked myself up off the ground, I understood the meaning of fortitude. Those opposing defensive lineman may have been bigger, but I learned that they couldn't compete with the size of my fight that was inside my small frame.

In life, there will be times where you'll have to put your ego aside and do the dirty work. You're not always going to have your ideal position and the fame that comes along with it. You may have to start at the bottom or at the bottom of a pile. You might have to take on a challenge that will take you out of your comfort zone. But that's better than standing on the sideline being a spectator. You can't learn anything about yourself if you don't challenge yourself. *How else are you gonna know what you're made of?*

Just remember, doing the dirty work is better than doing no work at all. To change the game and

your position in it, you first have to get in the game
and get your uniform dirty.

Don't Be Afraid To See The World

My junior and senior years of high school kept me busy ripping and running. I lettered in baseball, basketball and football, handled my schoolwork and worked on the weekend. I didn't even have time to have a steady girlfriend. I did manage to make it to a few house parties and a couple of movie times at the local movie theatre. Courtship or settling down was not a priority for me. I was too busy figuring out ways to make an honest dollar. My first job was at the Saratoga Café, washing dishes for a little money on the side. The café was a white only establishment so I did my job and ate my lunch in the back of the kitchen. I kept to myself. I only spoke when I was spoken to.

Then in the summer of 1951, I worked as a bellhop for the Denison Hotel. In that position, I only said a couple of words, mainly "Thank you sir and thank you ma'am." Every time I heard that bell ring, I was thinking tips. I was making some decent pocket change, so I didn't complain. Although, I'd rather be making some big folding money. Being a bellhop was definitely better than washing dishes, but neither job gave me much of a future in Denison.

With only weeks left in my senior year and graduation quickly approaching, I was contemplating life after high school. *What am I gonna do? Will I spend the rest of my life in Denison?* I had talks with baseball scouts, but I never heard the right words that would make me want to pursue a professional career. Getting a job at the Perrin Air Force Base located between Sherman and Denison was an option, but deep down inside I wanted to leave town to explore opportunities that I knew Denison couldn't provide. Fortunately, my mother understood my desire to leave Denison and she was very supportive. She gave me no pressure to stick around and I was grateful to have her blessing. I had to live my life and see what the world had to offer. She was also aware that the friction between my stepfather and me was like rubbing two pieces of sandpaper together. Sooner or later, one of us was gonna snap and our animosity would lead to a physical altercation. Out of respect for my mother, I didn't want her to witness that.

There was a phrase that resonated and echoed throughout the halls of Terrell High. It was always in my ear, and all the young people in Denison heard it on the radio at one time or another:

JOIN THE NAVY, SEE THE WORLD

It was an effective slogan. It was stuck in my

head. I couldn't shake the words, "See the world."

In downtown, there was a Navy recruiting station, so at 17, I went down there and signed my name on the dotted line. Almost immediately, I had boarded a bus that was leaving Denison on its way to Dallas. On August 29, 1951, at the Armed Forces recruiting center, I took an oath and I was sworn into the Navy.

Before I knew it, I was on a train to San Diego's Naval Training Center. I didn't know what to expect, but I wasn't afraid. I was ready to see the world.

U.S. Navy Training Center
San Diego, California. (1951)

What's In A Name?

My first day aboard the USS *Philippine Sea*, a sailor named Henry Blunt immediately started calling me Red. Around that time, my hair color was "sandy red", and my skin tone was what you would call "*red bone*", so you can say, the nickname was appropriate. Word traveled throughout my division and from that day on, I was officially known as Red. My first name Harold became an afterthought. At first, I wasn't comfortable with a fellow sailor giving me a nickname. But once I heard the nicknames of other sailors like Slim, Bighead, and Shorty, I was more than okay with Red.

I couldn't deny that being called Red had a "ring" to it—it's catchy. But make no mistakes, I wasn't looking for extra attention, and I had no intention on trying to win a popularity contest. The Navy is not the place to exercise your individualism. The Commanding Officers didn't care about my "catchy" little nickname. They were more concerned about the character and integrity I had behind the nickname. At 17, when you're more inclined to do and see things your way, they wanted to know if I had the maturity and discipline to follow Navy protocol. Once I put on my sailor uniform, I quickly learned that there was only one way to do things:

THERE'S THE RIGHT WAY, THE WRONG WAY, AND THE NAVY WAY

In the Navy, good conduct did not only consist of the words that came out of your mouth, but also how you carried yourself. Body language was just as important as the language you spoke. Standing upright, looking an officer in the eye and giving a sailor's salute with the right hand, spoke volumes about the values you hold close to your chest. The expectations were clear—accountability, commitment and having honor was the Navy way. Along with my uniform, my name was now representing my country, my fellow sailors and myself. And when your name is representing something, you'll quickly understand the power of your reputation.

A reputation can do many things. It can be the introduction to a good conversation or it can carry some baggage you might not want to deal with. One day, I can be Red, the sailor proclaimed to be the *life of the party*. The next day, I'm rumored to be a backstabbing sailor that will betray you at the drop of a dime. A reputation can easily be on the tip of everyone's tongue.

"You heard of that guy they call Red?"

"Yeah, I heard he doesn't stay on the straight and narrow. I was told you have to feed him with a long handled spoon."

"You know what they say, catch a lie, find a thief."

That's why you should focus more attention to your reputation than the "ring" of your name. Your reputation is built on what you do and what you stand for. I wanted to be known for doing my job and representing the high moral standards of the Navy. Horseplay and goofing around was not my thing. During the Korean War, my reputation was on the line. We were in uniform fighting under the same flag, and all that mattered was your performance.

In the heat of battle, I was below deck the USS *Philippine Sea*, wiping sweat from my forehead as I sent up ammunition to the hanger deck. Then from the hanger deck, sailors busted their behinds to quickly move the ammunition to the flight deck, where it was finally loaded onto the jet planes. Everyone had a job to do and it had to be executed in seconds. There was no room for error. Everything came down to who you could trust to do the job. I had to trust that the sailor next to me was going to do his part while I did mine. I took care of my business—that's what they can say about Red.

Nowadays I understand with this thing called "social media" everyone wants to establish a reputation for themselves. Today, you can create an account, add a name and project whatever image you want to your followers. I didn't grow up in a virtual world. When it came to my reputation, I didn't have technology to rely on—my name had to carry the weight. I grew up with the simple principle that what you talked about, you had to be about. That principle still applies and it always will.

Invest time in your character, preserve your integrity and value honesty, and a good reputation will follow. That's the foundation that makes a name. And hopefully, when you leave this earth people will respect and remember yours.

You can see why my fellow sailors called me Red.
Nimitz Beach, Kalaeloa, HI. (1953)

Ignorance Has No Limits, And Neither Does Your Resilience

When it came to life aboard the USS *Philippine Sea*, I was so occupied with work I don't even remember observing the waters of the ocean. There were three divisions of sailors, and all three worked in rotation around the clock. For every job you can imagine, a sailor was hard at work performing those duties the Navy way. When my division was given time off, which was appropriately called "liberty," we all stormed the foreign shores to explore the land.

I will never forget the time I was in Japan. With all the exotic food and sightseeing possibilities, I found myself in the middle of the dance floor. I was doing the jitterbug and my lady friend was following my every lead. While we were shuffling our feet to the beat, she began to circle around me. I started to smile. I thought she wanted to get a glimpse of my firm backside. But the problem was she never circled back around. I looked over my shoulder and to my surprise she had stopped dancing. She was standing still and staring directly at my backside. By her blank expression, I could tell this was not a flattering situation. She looked confused. And now, I was too. I started to notice that she wasn't the only one that had some screws loose. I scanned the dance floor and I could point out seven girls that were doing the same. They were all staring at the backsides of my buddies. They were waiting for something to happen. We all just looked at each other in utter amazement. I was thinking to myself, "I can't wait to get back home to the ladies in the States. These ladies here are crazy."

The next morning, I could tell that the story had already made its rounds throughout the ship. There was a lot of grumbling among the sailors. But I still didn't hear any explanation for those ladies strange behavior until a sailor pulled me to the side and gave me the scoop. The white servicemen from our US Armed Forces told the Japanese women that after midnight, like werewolves at a full moon, black men transform into monkeys with furry tails. *Do you believe that?* You better believe it. I wish I could tell you this was fiction, that this was some crude joke. It was not.

The truth is, racism was alive and well. Even though blacks and whites served under the same red, white and blue flag, the underlying belief was we were not equal. Instead of those white servicemen shining a light of brotherhood and unity, they decided to take the liberty to create a cloud of bigotry.

Always remember, underneath the spread of

ignorance lies the truth and you can't run from the truth. People won't always reveal their true intentions. They may try to mask the truth and deceive you with hatred and fear. The truth is, those white servicemen wanted all the ladies for themselves, and they figured spreading racial lies would prevent a charming, handsome man like myself, from enjoying my liberties.

That day I learned that ignorance has no limits. And in life, there are people that do not want you to succeed. That person may be wearing the same uniform as you. They may appear to be on your side, but behind their smile is a desire to see you fail.

There are many people in this world that are so consumed by fear and insecurities that nothing makes them happier than to see you get caught up in their mess. They want you to see the world from their narrow and limited point of view. They secretly want you to join their ranks of small-mindedness.

It's a cold, cold world, so dress warm. You're gonna face some bullcrap in life. I'm not only talking about racism, it can be sexism, ageism or any other type of 'ism. You will have to withstand any amount of hate that comes your way. Believe me, it can and will come from anywhere. Know who you are and don't be defined by the ignorance of others. Always stand tall, stick your chest out and don't let anything lead you astray from your rightful path. Continue to listen to the music of resilience—keep dancing, enjoy yourself and tell that ignorant person to kiss your tail.

Allow Yourself To Be Taken Under Someone's Wing, So You Can Learn How To Take Flight

When I was honorably discharged from the Navy on May 29, 1955, I knew I was embarking on a new chapter in life. I was 21 years old, and I had to decide whether I was going to stay in San Diego or travel to a new location to live. I didn't mind establishing myself in San Diego. The weather was absolutely beautiful, and it was a big city full of opportunity. Even though I had no idea of what career path I would follow. I did know that moving back to Denison was not an option. I made the leap and I felt that returning back home would be a step back. I wanted to continue moving forward to a brighter horizon. I just needed a little guidance to see it.

I was fortunate enough to have my cousin Herman and his wife Ruth take me under their wing. Herman offered me a room for $60 a month and I quickly accepted—that was a darn good deal!

I got a full-time job waiting tables at The Kona Kai Club on Shelter Island, across from the San Diego Lindbergh Field Airport. It was an honest paycheck, so I couldn't complain. However, if my pockets were fatter, I wouldn't have had a problem with that either.

One day, I told Herman that I was looking for a new job. He started talking about the ins and outs of his job as a carpenter. In conversation, he showed me a quick look at his paycheck and my eyes lit up. Not only was it honest, but the pay was significantly more. That's all I needed to see. The next day I joined the Carpenters Union and I enrolled as a student at San Diego City College. Through their 4-year apprenticeship program, I attended night classes and I learned everything I could about carpentry. And I mean everything, how to draft plans, cut roofs, prepare layouts, frame houses, and estimate the cost of a project.

When I became a member of the union, Herman set out to find me a working partner. He hoped to find somebody with experience and a willingness to teach a young man the craft. Both were important, but the latter was an exception. There weren't many keen on volunteering to be a mentor.

With a stroke of good luck, there was an older man named Austin Lucious who happened to be working by himself. While a jack-of-all-trades, Austin's specialty was roof stacking. We set up a deal. I would pick him up every morning at 7:00 a.m. and in return, he would teach me everything he knew about carpentry. We hit it off. I had the right attitude and I was willing to listen. Austin was patient and ready to teach—that combination is a powerful thing.

Under his wing, I absorbed everything like a sponge. We worked every day from 8 to 5, and I went to night school two nights a week on top of that. I was able to combine my experience on the construction site with my curriculum from the classroom. I kept Austin occupied with questions and within two months, I thought we were an excellent team.

Early one morning, I picked up Austin and as soon as I saw his face, I could tell he wasn't feeling too well. While driving, it looked like he was suffering from an upset stomach. Right when we arrived at the construction site, Austin turned to me and said, "I don't think I can go today. I'm gonna sit this one out. Can you handle the job?"

I told him, "I can handle it."

Our job was to stack the roof, so I immediately had to get to work. I started putting up all the rafters on top of the house. I installed the wooded braces, nailed the collar ties to the rafters, and then I put in the freeze blocks and the vents at the plate line of the house. Lastly, I installed the gable end vents at the end of the house—the roof was officially stacked.

I was dead tired as I walked slowly to the car to check on Austin. Although I felt exhausted, I was itching to get his opinion on the roof. To my surprise, I approached the car to find Austin laughing and grinning from ear to ear. *I was thinking, either I had something on my face or I did an exceptional job.* Through his laughter, he proceeded to explain...

Come to find out, he wasn't sick at all. It was a test. He was relaxing in the car, and with one eye open, he was observing my work. He wanted to see how much I learned and if I could handle the job by myself.

Well, I passed the test. I was ready to leave the nest. Austin, like any good mentor was wise enough to know when the time was right for me to take flight.

I was forever blessed to be under the wings of my cousin Herman and Austin. They provided me with a foundation and a career that helped me take flight as a man. With their guidance, I was able to stand on my own two feet and establish a life in San Diego. But I'm also grateful that I wasn't too prideful and hardheaded to except their guidance. I had the *eagerness* to allow them to take me under their wings.

Red Allen
San Diego, California. (1955)

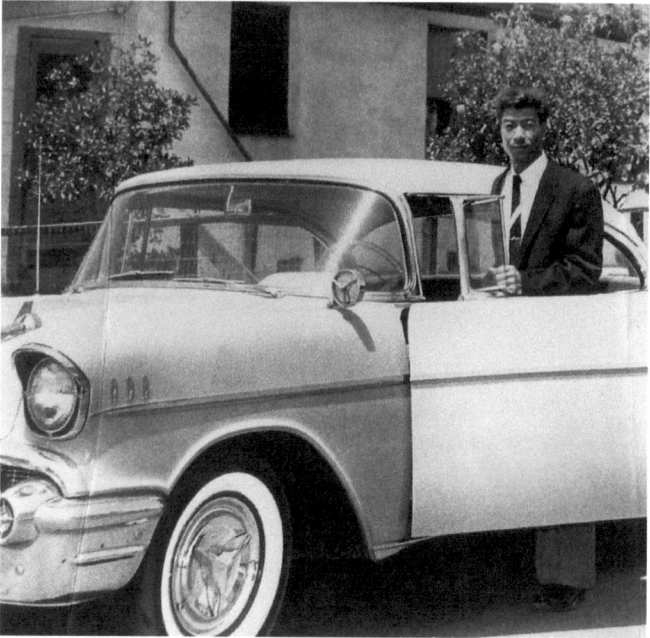

Say Hello To My Chevrolet Bel Air Sport Coupe

You Can't Be A King Without A Queen

Life was good in sunny San Diego and I didn't think it could get any better, but then I met Gwendolyn Johnson.

Herman and Ruth were members of Calvary Baptist Church. Before moving into Herman's house, it had been a long time since I stepped foot into a church. In the Navy, I might have read a couple of scriptures here and there, but nothing I would consider a Sunday service. I felt it would be a good time to reconnect with my heavenly father, so one Sunday I conveniently tagged along. After hearing the pastor's sermon, I knew I walked into the right place. I decided to make Calvary my home of worship. The day I joined, Reverend S. M. Lockridge asked me what church I attended in Denison. I told him I was a member of Hopewell Baptist Church and the pastor was Reverend L.B. George. He immediately smiled and said, "Reverend George, that's my buddy." I came to find out, they both went to Ministry School in Dallas. The next Sunday, I got baptized and I accepted Jesus Christ as my personal Lord and Savior.

In the first couple of months, I just sat

quietly with Herman and Ruth listening to the powerful words of every sermon. In between flipping through bible verses, the choir would do a number and have everyone on their feet, clapping and singing along. The room would fill with the Holy Spirit. One Sunday, this attractive girl, emerged from the choir to perform a gospel solo. She sang soprano and her voice was almost as beautiful as she was. Well, I did a little research and with Ruth's help, I got the scoop—her name was Gwendolyn Johnson. Her sister, Beverly sang alto in the choir. Her parents, Herbert and Alice Johnson were well known figures in the church. They were from New Orleans, and in 1952 they'd made San Diego their home. They both served as deacon and deaconess, Sunday school teachers in the Young People and Adult Department, and were both members of the Gospel and Sanctuary Choir.

Based on their position in the church, I knew that before I could try to sweet talk Gwendolyn I needed to be in her father's good graces. Luckily, when I met Herbert, I was able to make a quick connection. We shared a common bond—he was a plasterer by trade and he admired the fact that we both earned a living with our hands. I have to admit; it felt damn good to be a carpenter.

Herbert was what you would call a "man's man", a class act and a man of his word. He had a quiet confidence and caring heart that made everyone want to be around him. These were all characteristics that I strived to emulate.

Herbert had a gift for putting together the hottest gospel groups that New Orleans and San Diego had ever heard. He founded The Johnson Sisters, a group that included Gwendolyn, Beverly, and his sisters Lois, Bernetta, and Marion. When Gwendolyn and Beverly arrived with their parents at Calvary in 1953, they became a gospel duo called The Cavaliers. Then Herbert, with keen eye for talent, recruited Stella Snowden, Gloria Hullaby, Jean Wesson and Charles Ray Warren. The Cavaliers sang like a choir of angels. I was always in the crowd listening to The Cavaliers, and keeping an eye on Gwendolyn. She carried herself with class, and also being a fox didn't hurt one bit. My first move was to join the choir and make an impression, but that didn't work. I was stuck in the back row, in the tenor section, singing off key and mumbling the words. I would often try to grab her attention, but it seemed she only noticed the horrible notes that I sung. She was also an usher and every so often I would try to flash her a smile as she stood by the aisle, but even those little attempts of wooing didn't work.

The moment of truth came at a church picnic on the 4th of July in 1956, at El Monte Park. That's when I got my chance. I saw her standing in line waiting to grab some food so I eased my way right next to her. We both exchanged a quick glance and then I *officially* introduced myself.

"Hello, my name is Red Allen."

The fireworks exploded early that day—we talked for hours. I told her all about Denison and what brought me out to San Diego. From that moment on, we were inseparable. Cupid hit me in the heart with an arrow and I fell head over heels.

Like most men, we want to be the king of the castle. We have a desire to make a name for ourselves and leave a legacy for the world to admire. But when we get to a certain age and start to carry the weight of the world on our shoulders, we realize that ruling a kingdom is easier said than done. If you want to sit on a throne, you must accept the truth, that heavy is the head that wears the crown. It's no easy job. You quickly learn that it's tough to conquer life's responsibilities and it's tougher facing those battles alone on your throne. The burden is too much for any king to handle, but finding the right partner can lift your spirits.

Gwendolyn was a partner with the substance and strength I needed to battle the challenges that life would throw at me. She was also someone I could laugh with and enjoy the simple things in life. I'd found my queen and I become a better man. And I had a little more hop in my step—the responsibilities and burdens of life didn't seem so heavy.

As much as I wanted to carry myself as a king, you never know you are one until you're treated like one. I was treated like royalty. I was given respect and I was handed the crown.

On June 1, 1958, we got married at Calvary. On that day, Gwendolyn and I established a solid foundation built on faith and the commitment that with love we could rule our kingdom. People say that behind every great man is a great woman. The only thing I may add is that Gwendolyn has stood by my side instead of behind me. That's what queens do.

For you future kings out there, here are some words of wisdom from my castle: *It's Better To Be Treated Like A King By One Woman, Than To Be Treated Like A Pawn By Ten.*

Mr. and Mrs. Allen

Happy Wife, Happy Life

A House Is Not A Home

After Gwendolyn and I walked down the aisle, I carried her across the threshold of our new house on 3705 Clinton Street. Our first goal was to start a family and it didn't take us long. In less than a year, on March 9th, Harold Jr. was born. Then a year later, on March 26th, Marcus was born. I knew in time, our house on Clinton Street would be too small to contain a growing family. It wasn't hard to envision a youthful Harold and Marcus running around the house, knocking things over and causing a stir.

In June of 1963, while grading and setting the forms on the foundation of a house, I learned that the property would soon become available on the market. The lady that owned it was behind on her taxes and she couldn't pay off her debt. I jumped on the opportunity, secured a loan and paid off the remainder of the balance on the property. The address was 1003 Winston Drive. Gwendolyn and I were excited and thrilled at the prospect of having a long drive way and a big backyard. I even think our dog King was anxious at the opportunity to roam a new neighborhood.

I quickly assembled a team and we started construction in mid-July. I had extra incentive to finish the house because my third son, Damon was on the way. I had Austin Lucious draw up the blueprint, Herbert Johnson did the plastering and a contractor named Hue Stackhouse added his expertise. I hired a plumber and an electrician, and then I played my part by taking care of all the framing, the windows, and the doors. We worked at a fast pace. Everyone worked as a team and shortly before Christmas, the house was complete.

I felt good. This would be a new chapter for the Allen family. But for some reason, I didn't celebrate. I didn't crack open a beer, sit back and admire the house. Most fathers would love to tell their kids that the house they live in was built with their father's hands. As a carpenter I could pat myself on the back and tell the world of my great job. But there was something inside forcing me to look at the big picture. *What was the big picture?*

After all the planning, designing and construction work, at the end of the day, all I did was build a structure. A carpenter can build a house, but not a home. As a father, I realized that my work was far from done.

The truth was that I could build this house from the ground up, only to have the foundation crumble from within. Like the saying goes, "A house divided against itself cannot stand." If I could not keep the family together, *what type of father would I be?*

I had work to do. I wanted my family to have a home.

Family First

Bring A Lunch, This Will Be An All-Day Job

If you're ready to earn the title of father and not just pin a nametag on your shirt, grab a hard hat and pack a lunch. Being a father is not a job where you get a pat on the back for showing up. This is an all-day job—I'm talking 24/7, 365 days a year. This isn't a negotiable matter. If you're fortunate to be given a day off, cherish it. I've never had one. Even "Father's Day" is a day where I still have to clock in.

Once you become a father, you will quickly learn your job has many titles, and it comes with many responsibilities that frankly, you won't be prepared for. You will be called on to be a historian, financial advisor, dating doctor, guidance counselor, athletic coach, and that's just for starters. Keep in mind, there is no degree at Father University that you can acquire to deal with this job. There is no instruction manual on how to handle the challenges that you will face.

As the years go by, and your kids become older, your role may be reduced. You may be lucky enough to get a hug and hear the words, "Job well done." Don't fall for it. Don't think for one second, you can retire, put on your gold watch and ride off into the sunset. Your presence is always needed. You will always be a father.

The Lord knows I have put on my hard hat and punched the clock every day. He also knows I have not always made the right moves. I have not always done and said the right things. There were always a couple more hugs that I could have given. I could have been more vocal when expressing my love. Considering all that, there is one thing I do know. I can look in the mirror and know that I was on the job. I was present.

Just like any full-time job, you have to show up, day in and day out. And we all know, your attendance is monitored. Kids always remember the days when you were absent. They never forget.

No one is perfect and I didn't bother trying to be. I don't wear wings and I never claimed to walk on water. I just did what I had to do—that was bring a lunch and show up every day.

(From left to right) Harold Jr., Marcus, Damon, Red, Michelle, Michael, Gwendolyn

(From left to right) Marcus, Red, Gwendolyn, Harold Jr., Michael (Seated) Damon, Michelle

(From left to right) Harold Jr., Michael, Damon, Marcus (Seated) Michelle, Darius, Gwendolyn, Red

A family that prays together stays together.
(From left to right) Michael, Harold Jr., Marcus, Red holding
Darius

The Apple Doesn't Fall Far From The Tree

I have six beautiful children, Harold Jr., Marcus, Damon, Michael, Michelle and my youngest, Darius. All my kids have their own personalities, which is good because I wanted them to be individuals. On the other hand, I do have to admit and be mindful that my kids are small mirrors reflecting different sides of my personality.

In life, we've all heard the saying, "The apple doesn't fall far from the tree." *What does that saying really mean?* When I think of the saying, I always imagine a father as a farmer planting a single apple tree. The farmer's goal is to grow healthy, well-rounded apples. He has the responsibility of holding the watering can and determining when and how much water should soak the roots of the tree. However, in this case the father is like a farmer watering the "family tree". A father's daily words, actions and demeanor are the water sprinkling at the base.

We fathers must remember that not only is our DNA in our kids, our approach to parenting and nurturing molds them into the people they become. It's the combination of nature and nurture. My outlook, behavior and attitude towards life have shaped my kids, for the good and for the bad—it is what it is. I definitely do not control their every action and I can't determine the final destination of their journeys, but I can influence whether they travel their journeys with optimism or pessimism. I always saw the glass half full. In fact, my goal was to fill it to the top. I wanted my kids to share that same goal. I told my kids that they could achieve anything as long as they worked hard and believed in themselves. That's the water that was in my can.

This is why it is important to be at your *best* as a father. Most fathers come to the realization that you never know which bits and pieces of yourself will manifest in your kids. I hope this is the anxiety that new fathers feel, when they start to examine themselves as a man and decide what type of father they want to be. The anxiety that causes fathers-to-be to ask themselves the tough questions. *What will I teach my kids? How do I raise a kid that will make smart decisions? What traits do I have that I do not want my kids to inherit?*

Like I said, a father has many job titles and farmer can be added to the list. Although I have tried my best to distribute the water evenly at the roots, certain traits and qualities that I exhibited as a farmer have borne fruit that has not fallen far from my tree. I would like to think that at my best, these are the qualities that I've produced in my apple barrel.

Harold Jr. was born on March 9, 1959.

Giving a son your first name is the equivalent of starting a race and passing the baton to the next runner to carry the next leg. I passed the baton to Harold Jr. and he ran off with my leadership qualities. We're both firstborns and we were naturally the first option when family needed a helping hand. As the oldest of the siblings, Harold had to take the lead—there was no one to follow. He was the first to be given the rules of the house— good grades, chores, curfew—and he was the first to execute them. Harold would become the first in the Allen family to obtain a college degree, a B.A in Political Science from Whittier College. It is only fitting that he would be the first to catch the coaching bug, roaming the sidelines and the dugouts coaching his two sons.

Marcus was born March 26, 1960. At an early age, he quickly picked up my studious side. I always found time at home to analyze blueprints and study my craft. As a carpenter, I had to be exact with measurements, precise with the placement of parts, and consistent with every task. Marcus took that same attention to detail and diligence to the game of football. Marcus did not only rely on his talent and his natural aggressiveness, he studied his craft. Even at the youth level of football, Marcus became a student of the game. He learned the responsibility of each player on both sides of the ball. When he watched football on television, he would call plays as if he was on the sideline coaching. He approached the game with a quarterback's mentality and the heart of a linebacker. From the first day he found his passion, Marcus was aware that for him to be one of the greats, he had to understand the x's and o's.

Damon was born on July 29, 1963. He reflects my independent side. Damon had to pave his own way and be an individual in a growing family. When Damon finished his record-breaking football career along with winning a College World Series Championship at Cal State Fullerton in 1984, he was faced with a major decision. He could play baseball in the minor league system for the Detroit Tigers or take his talent to Canada and play quarterback. When I was faced with the decision to stay in my hometown of Denison or broaden my horizons by joining the Navy, I knew that decision was a monumental one, but my independent spirit would not allow me to second guess my intuition. Defining my life and who I would become was up to me, and I could not be afraid to make that step. Damon was also unafraid to take that step, board a plane to Canada and create his own legacy in the Canadian Football League.

Michael and Michelle, born 3 minutes apart on January 31, 1965, are the twins of the family. And when they were growing up, every 3 minutes Gwendolyn and I had to keep our eyes on them. The twins quickly asserted themselves into the family tree.

Michael, fell right into the mix of things, joining the ranks of his active brothers. Michael was quick to put on the Encanto uniform, compete and perform. Michael mirrors my sociable side. He has a zest for photography and behind each photo is his love for life. Smiling, laughing and appreciating every day with family and friends is something that we all should embrace. He wears his heart on his sleeve and everywhere he goes, that camera is with him documenting life and those precious moments that we hold close to our hearts. Michael is not the writer of the family, but he's always known that a picture is worth a thousand words.

Michelle, my only daughter, represents my competitive side. She had to hold her own when dealing with the boys. After years of keeping up with her brothers, Michelle developed only one gear: full speed. When she puts her mind to something, she has an intensity that is only matched by her own enthusiasm to win. At Lincoln High, she was the Female Athlete of the Year in 1983, lettering in softball, basketball and volleyball. Whether we're talking a game of dominoes, spades or deciding to return to school to further her education, Michelle's competitive drive is second to none. We both feel that if you're presented with a challenge, you must take it on and give 110% from start to finish. There's no other option.

Darius was born on October 1, 1977. I jokingly refer to him as *The Last of the Mohicans*. He was in the privileged position to hear all the stories of my life and the family's. All my books, philosophies and quotes have been passed down to him. The memories of my travels and The Berenstain Bears were his bedtime stories. The tales of the Negro Leagues and all my sports heroes were shared over fishing trips. It is no surprise he is a screenwriter, sports historian, and an author. He naturally picked up my storytelling side—and we all love a well-told story.

Teamwork Starts In The Home

Before our kids would learn about John McKay's USC Trojans, Red Auerbach's Boston Celtics and Vince Lombardi's Green Bay Packers, Gwendolyn and I wanted our kids to know about the #1 team in Southeast San Diego. We wanted to be their first example of a winning team. Giving your kids a living example of teamwork is the best way to teach them the importance of working together to achieve a common goal. It is one thing to say, "family first" and it's another thing, to show it. As a team, our goal was to be active in our kids' lives, and we knew that clear communication and teamwork were at the heart of achieving that goal.

Even though my job as a carpenter and her job as a vocational nurse allowed us little time to relax, we still found time to attend every Sunday service at Calvary, every choir rehearsal, every booster club meeting, and all school PTA meetings.

When I coached at Encanto Little League and Southeastern Pop Warner, Gwendolyn was the team mom and if I wasn't coaching, we both were in the stands supporting our kids. No matter the distance, we traveled to see every ballgame and function.

If Gwendolyn couldn't cook her signature New Orleans style red beans and rice or the family favorite, gumbo, consequently I was in the kitchen with my recipes. Although, my selections—chitlins, my version of Lemons Café's chili and menudo—weren't too popular around the house.

All in all, we were quite the duo. If I could sing, I believe we would give Marvin Gaye and Tammi Terrell a run for their money.

Through thick and thin, the ups and downs, and despite our busy schedules, Gwendolyn and I made it happen. That's what good teams do—perform under adversity, execute the game plan and win.

The 1972 Encanto Little League Braves
(Back row) Second to left, Gwendolyn next to Marcus; Second
to far right, Red

If You Can't See The World, Bring The World To Your Kids

Our kids didn't grow up privileged. Although they were rich in love and support, financially, we had to master the art of stretching a dollar. When I served my home cooked chili, silver spoons weren't used to scoop up the chunks of meat. We just used ordinary bowls and flatware. We didn't take cross country road trips or annual family vacations to Europe. There weren't many passports floating around the house. For our kids to see the world, we had to bring them the world. With our limited resources, we provided basic but essential ways to expose them to a world beyond our street address.

We may have lived in the city, but our backyard resembled parts of Denison. Like they say, "You can take the kid out the country, but you can't take the country out of the kid." Through the years, we've had several breeds of dogs, a slow walking turtle, two loud mouth geese, a flock of wandering chickens and 2 Shetland ponies. I also had a horse at the Bayview Baptist Church stables. Gwendolyn sometimes protested my penchant for collecting animals, but the kids never complained. For a period of time, I even managed to have some muddy pigs rolling around the backyard, even though they were not permissible in city limits.

I set up a mini library so their minds could explore. It was stacked with books on Black History, world events, sports, science fiction, mathematics, and enough Encyclopedia Britannicas to fill a closet. And I can't forget about the Bible. Musically, we had records from Motown, Gospel, Jazz and my favorite, the Blues. I introduced them to Bobby "Blue" Bland, but I think his subject matter was too much to digest at the time.

The most interesting item I had in the house was a drug-identification kit. It was a circular case that when spun, it revealed a transparent window displaying every popular drug in the land. Gwendolyn and I made sure that our kids knew what marijuana, heroin and cocaine could do to their dreams. In life, drugs don't take the backseat, they take the steering wheel. If you want to go places, you're gonna have to decide who's driving— you or the drugs.

If they wanted to experiment with drugs, I gave them permission to do it right there in the house. We knew that wasn't happening.

Gwendolyn and I didn't have the luxury of the Internet. Parents today can just purchase a computer and a smartphone, allowing their kids to have the world at their fingertips. *The question is are kids taking advantage of these tools? What are they learning about the world? Are they wasting time online and on their phones?* Even with Internet access and the technology to travel the world without a passport, kids can still be stuck on the same website address.

In this day and age, there's no excuse, make sure kids' minds are traveling the world.

If I Don't Know The Parents, Don't Bring Your Friends Around

My kids had rules that they needed to abide by, and if their friends were at my house, they would have to fall right in line with my standards. It was mandatory that I not only had a relationship with their friend's parents, the parents needed to have a clear understanding of what I stood for. I wanted them to know exactly where I was coming from.

If you don't know the parents, issues can arise when you need to chastise a kid's behavior. Kids may cross the line and you'll step in to discipline them, but then you might have to step back and consider what their parents would think. The kid and their parents could take offense to your words and actions.

I surely wouldn't want any parents disciplining my kids without my approval, but then again at every house that my kids hung out at, I knew the parents. They were just a phone call away. I had their respect and they had mine. I did not have a problem with any stand up parent making sure my kids behaved properly. During my day, there was a community agreement that if any kid was getting too big for their britches, any parent had the license to discipline them. Times sure have changed.

A Dog Is A Family's Best Friend

Out of all the pets that have become members of the family, there is only one that left a permanent paw print on our hearts. Even today, the very mention of his name brings back memories just like flipping through a family photo album. That name is King. We brought him with us on our move from Clinton Street to Winston Drive. King was a highly intelligent, brown and black German Shepherd with a passion for hopping fences and winning staring contests. Athletic and energetic, King was the perfect dog for an active family like ours. He was forever obedient and overly protective and for that, the family absolutely loved him. It just so happens; we gave him the perfect name.

Back in the early '60s, around my part of town, dogs weren't relegated to the backyard. Dogs had more freedom. It was no surprise to see a pack of dogs roaming the streets. I'm talking stray dogs, pets or a mixture of both. Dogs had their own town hall meetings and it didn't take long to see that King was the neighborhood alpha dog. No trash can was to be ransacked and no fire hydrant was to be peed on without an okay "bark" from King.

However, when you're the King, someone is

always after your throne. Right above our house, lived the Thompson family. A warm family that always had an open door policy. For our kids, it was their second home. Too bad, King and the Thompson's German Shepherd Mustang didn't share the same love. The only thing they shared was their natural instinct to be territorial. Whenever they crossed paths, they fought to see who the biggest and baddest German Shepherd in the neighborhood was. Their fights were so intense that we had to grab the water hose to separate them. Now this is nothing to glorify, but King was our protector to the fullest extent.

King, like most dogs exemplified the true meaning of loyalty. Through thick and thin, a dog will protect you and be with you till the very end. A dog will never leave your side. Even if you have no food to eat, your dog will sit there and starve with you.

Think to yourself, how often do you see a homeless person with a cat? Let's be honest, if a cat is not fed, a cat will eventually take off, just as quick as you can say, "Meow." Not a dog. That's why a dog is a man's best friend. A dog will surely show you their puppy-dog eyes. You'll hear their whimpers, but no matter the circumstances that dog will stay by your side.

King was the family's best friend, a daily reminder of loyalty and dependability. King was a source of unwavering joy. In a world full of uncertainty, one thing was for certain—we could depend on King's drooling tongue and wagging tail whenever he was around. We could depend on King to protect us. That's a wonderful thing. There's comfort in that.

King died of old age, but his memory has never left our family's hearts and minds.

It Is Their Passion, Not Yours

Although I have a passion for sports and I sometimes reminisce about those days when I got my uniform dirty at Terrell High, I did not set out to create an athletic family. I never positioned my kids to play sports thinking one day it might bring the Allen name fortune and fame. To be honest, I just wanted to keep my kids busy. Gwendolyn and I are firm believers that idle hands are the devil's tools. In addition to their schoolwork, we had them involved in piano lessons, church choir, trumpet lessons, boy scouts, cub scouts, martial arts, hunting, fishing and camping. Not to mention, softball, Pop Warner football, Little League baseball and even basketball.

Not only did these activities keep them out of trouble, it allowed them a way to find their own passions in life. With all those activities, they were bound to find something they liked and disliked.

There was simply no way I was going to be unfair to my kids by forcing them to live out my dreams. Any thoughts I had of what could have been were left back in Denison. I always told my kids they could be whatever they wanted, but I never insisted that I needed a doctor, lawyer or a football player in the family. That's not how you do it. It's definitely not the way to keep the fire burning on your kid's true passion. Believe me, if your kid is not focused on their desires, their drive will burn out pursuing yours. You may think you're igniting a fire, but you're really just lighting a candle.

It may surprise you to learn that when I asked Harold and Marcus if they wanted to sign up to play Little League baseball, their answer was, "No". Even though they were swinging the baseball bat down the street, playing with the Jackson brothers, Monte, Terry and David, they had no interest. I didn't spend time trying to persuade them either. If their heart wasn't in it, then it just wasn't in it. Once they said "No", I figured that was more time for me to possibly relax and enjoy a beer.

The only thing that changed their minds was a visit from a neighborhood friend, Lauren Kuykendall. He came by the house, dressed in his uniform, looking like a young Maury Wills. Next thing I know, I was coaching my kids baseball team, the Encanto Braves.

The World Needs More Orange Trucks

When I run into former players that I coached in Little League and Pop Warner, they jokingly ask me, "Mr. Allen, where's that orange truck?"

I smile and think back to 1970 when I made one of the best purchases of my life, a bright orange Chevy CST-10 pickup truck. When I first drove the car off the lot, my primary intention was to use the truck for construction work but somehow its main service was public transportation. I had no idea the color orange, would in time represent hope and provide a lasting memory for so many in Southeast San Diego.

Like many coaches in youth sports, after practices and games I would provide players with a ride home. I didn't think it was a big deal. I just felt it was a coach's duty.

At the time I was not fully aware of the impact, but apparently my orange pickup brought smiles to kids faces like a neighborhood ice cream truck. Instead of 10-cent popsicles and the catchy music, my truck was packed with kids who loved to ride in the back as we flew through the city streets.

Reminiscing about those days, it was quite

daring to have kids in the back of the truck hanging onto the rail. One evening, a police officer pulled me over and told me, "Mr. Allen, you're doing a great job, but you have to slow it down, especially with these energetic kids in the back." He could have easily given me a ticket, but he just gave me a warning. I think the officer was a former little leaguer and remembered those glory days of getting a ride home after games.

Gladly, times have changed and safety is a priority, but the significance of filling up your gas tank and scooping up your players will never change. For many, that orange truck did not only represent a ride, it was a symbol of support, self-worth and a sense of community. I enjoyed making sure a kid knew that their contribution was vital to the team's success.

Although, I no longer have that orange truck, there are many orange trucks across the world and guess what? We need more.

Don't get caught up in titles—you can be a Little League coach, a mentor, a role model, a big brother or a big sister. No matter what's on your nametag, extend your hand as far as you can and help someone. We all know no man is an island, and we're all part of one big team with one coach.

There were many times where my kids became jealous and wondered, "Why don't the other kids get their *own* father?"

Now that my kids are older, they understand

that some issues are bigger than them. They weren't losing their father; they were learning how to become a better person and a team player on a bigger field. They now realize the need to extend a helping hand and they know there is more than enough space for others in the back of the orange truck.

The Orange Truck

It's Never Too Late Or Too Early To Call A Family Meeting

I've heard some disturbing news. A little bird told me that today's fathers are not utilizing one of the most effective tools in the tool shed. When it comes to keeping a family together and your kids in line, this tool can do the job. I'm talking about the "family meeting".

Just like in football and basketball, the use of the huddle is key for a team's success. Whether the coach needs to draw up a winning play or implement a new game plan, a huddle is an effective way to get everyone on the same page.

The same goes for the family. Every now and then, a father needs to call a family meeting to gather everyone together and go over the expectations. I've called many family meetings in my day. And if I needed to call one today, I wouldn't hesitant to pull out my little phone book. It's the best way to connect with your kids, and it gives them a platform where they can voice their opinions. Even though I was the presiding judge, if they had any issues to put on the table, I gave everyone the opportunity to state their case. Keep in mind; my courtroom didn't entertain too many cases.

The family meeting could be weekly, monthly or as frequently as needed. I borrowed my style from the Navy—I was all about the element of surprise.

The topics varied—one day I'm reminding my kids who paid the bills in the house, and on another day, I'm telling them to stop fussing and fighting. But there was one topic that I had to discuss during numerous family meetings—chores! My kids were no strangers to having chores and the least favorite by far, was dish washing. They didn't mind eating up all the food, but they absolutely tried their best to avoid anything to do with dirty dishes.

I gave each kid dish washing duty for the week and on this particular night, Damon was on the job (or that's what I thought). I woke up in the middle of the night to grab something to drink. I walked into the kitchen, and flipped on the light switch to see a pile of dirty dishes stacked on the counter. I don't know what Damon was thinking, but I was about to find out.

So around midnight on a school night, I woke everyone up and called a surprise family meeting. I didn't care about the time. In fact, if I heard that anyone was asleep in the classroom because of my midnight meeting that would be grounds for a new family meeting.

I had the kids seated at the dinner table

wiping sleep out of their eyes, as they watched Damon wash the dishes. I wanted everyone to get a good look, so they wouldn't get any bright ideas on skipping their chores. Gwendolyn sat quietly to the side as I lectured them on the importance of taking care of their responsibilities. I personally let Damon know the dangers of procrastination. I told Damon that he has to, "Make hay while the sun shines."

"What does that mean?"

"That means, don't put something off for tomorrow that you can take care of today. Especially, something you were supposed to do...like these dishes. If you did them after dinner, we'd all be sleep right now."

Damon got the point and I can't tell you how relieved he was finishing that stack of dishes—we all were.

If You Don't Have Any Money, You Have No Business Going Into A Store

I had a saying that I would express to my kids, "If you don't have any money, you have no business going into a store." It was a saying that they became quite familiar with. Think about it, what good can come about walking into a store with no money to spend? Who really wants to go to a store to window shop? The only thing you'll spend is time dreaming about something you can't buy and most times, it's an item that you don't need. And for some, that temptation to possess can be too much to handle. Unfortunately, not everyone has grown up hearing that saying.

One afternoon, Damon, Michael and a neighborhood friend decided to walk to the local Thrifty's Drug Store to get some ice cream cones and junk food. Back in those days, Thrifty's provided more than prescription drugs. They provided any and everything you can think of, and the ice cream selection made it a popular destination for every kid in the community. The ice cream trucks that rolled around mainly sold popsicles and Mexican candies. Thrifty's was our neighborhood Baskin-Robbins. The only catch was that we didn't have 31 flavors to choose from, but we didn't mind. The biggest dilemma was whether to get a double or triple scoop ice cream cone. That tough decision made a long walk seem like a couple of steps for ice cream lovers.

Once they stepped foot into the store, Damon followed Michael to the potato chips section while their friend went directly to the candy aisle. He waited as Michael took his precious time going through all the flavors of Ruffles potato chips, which all seemed to be his favorite. Damon was only concerned with one thing—a double scoop of orange sherbet ice cream dripping on a cone.

Suddenly, the store manager yelled, "Hey kid, what are you doing?" Damon and Michael froze. They shared a concerned look as they both realized the voice was headed to another aisle. They slowly walked around to the next aisle to see the manager forcing their friend to empty his pockets. To their surprise, while they were busy figuring out ways to spend every cent they had, their friend was picking up goodies on the five-finger discount.

Damon and Michael didn't know what to think. Were the police on the way or worse, was I gonna show up? They had no idea their friend was low on cash—and it was already too late to discuss it. He was caught red-handed. As they looked at their friend, they thought about my saying, and how those words manifested at that very moment.

Luckily, the manager told them to scram. Damon and Michael could have been charged with being accomplices to their friend's attempt to break the law. They quickly took off, not waiting one second for that manager to second-guess his decision.

They were lucky the manager decided not to call the police. I can just see it now. The police officer telling the kid my prophetic words, "If you don't have any money, you have no business going into a store."

The Student Makes The School, The School Doesn't Make The Student

In the early '70s, the high schools in San Diego were segregated. Don't get tripped up by the Brown v. Board of Education ruling in 1954. The policy in San Diego was that students had to attend their neighborhood high school. Color lines divided the neighborhoods, so in a roundabout way segregation was still in effect.

The word around San Diego was that Abraham Lincoln High was a "rough school". Lincoln, also known as "The Hive" because of its mascot, the hornet, was our neighborhood high school. Like many schools across the nation, Lincoln had its issues with drugs and gang activity. So much that some families in the neighborhood would submit a different home address to other schools so that their kid can receive an education anywhere else besides Lincoln. Gwendolyn and I had no plans on changing our address. Despite Lincoln's reputation, it also had its share of bright students determined be successful despite their "rough" environment.

I understand from an economic standpoint that all schools are not created equal. Schools do not have the same budget and the same amount of resources. However it's important to realize that the greatest resource that a school has is the student itself. Great minds and talents can be found in any neighborhood.

As a father, all I needed to see was a faculty of caring, hard working individuals that were committed to bringing out the best in every student. It was my job to deliver a student with an appetite to learn. I felt strongly that those faculty members were at Lincoln High School: *Payton Cook, Principal; Colbert Williams, Janice Winston, Patricia Hyde, Ruth Rowe, Eugene Davis, Rudy Anderson, Harold Moore and Janet Singleton, Counselors; Louise Pearson, Stephanie Baron, Peggy Funches, Ida Hardy, Teachers; and Vic Player, Roy Reed, Richard Smith, Gary Flisher, Lou Courtney, Mel Washington and Skip Coons, Coaches.*

My kids had a strong foundation that would allow them to excel right there in the neighborhood.

In 1975, the San Diego Unified School District started busing kids from Southeast San Diego to schools throughout the county. Harold decided for his sophomore year that he wanted to wake up early every morning at 5:15 a.m. and catch a school bus to attend Patrick Henry High School. I don't recall signing any paperwork and right under my nose, Harold left the Hornets nest and became a Patriot.

Although, I would prefer kids from the Southeast to stay in the neighborhood, I could never knock a parent for wanting their kid to receive the best education possible. I just had my personal views on education as a whole:

1) Regardless of whether you go to your neighborhood school or one outside your district, self-education is the course that should last a lifetime. You can't solely depend on the school system to give you all the tools you need to survive. There is history that you will have to learn outside of your history class. There is life outside the textbook. The goal is to be book smart and street smart.

2) When it comes to getting bused out of the neighborhood, keep in mind that the grass isn't always greener on the other side. You can escape challenges at one school just to encounter some new ones at your next.

Harold learned that at Patrick Henry, the grass was not greener. Along with waking up early enough to crow with the roosters, Harold was having a tough time juggling schoolwork and football. After each practice, Harold would have to wait late in the evening to catch the city bus back home. He would enter the house around 8:00 p.m. as tired as a hound dog. The daily grind was becoming too much to handle. He wanted to go to Patrick Henry to be more productive, but with his new routine it became counterproductive to getting a better education.

Harold and I had a sit-down, and we decided that immediately after he'd complete his first semester, he was gonna return home to "The Hive". On the last day of the semester, I made a phone call to let the faculty know I was coming on campus to pick up my son. I met with the Principal who expressed that Harold was performing well academically, and that he should stay at Patrick Henry.

I said, "If he can do it here, he can do it at Lincoln. Have a good day."

If you can do something great, why not start within your neighborhood? You might face an uphill battle with the odds stacked against you, but the impact you can make will last forever. My kids were inspired and looked up to many great students at Lincoln, those who set a high standard academically and athletically.

As a student, you have the power to put your school on the map or you can put a black eye on the reputation of your school. The choice is yours.

Follow My Footsteps Or Choose Your Own Path

One weekend, I decided to bring Harold, Marcus and Damon to work with me. They were now in their teens and they were quickly approaching adulthood. I thought it would be a good time to remind them that they had to think about their futures and what they wanted to make of themselves.

If any of them had ambitions of following in my footsteps as a carpenter versus choosing their own path, this would be the ideal time to speak up.

At that time, I had a contracting job building an office in a wrecking yard in Otay Mesa, a community in the southern part of San Diego. I couldn't have chosen a better day to put them to work. It was 100 degrees outside, a perfect day to see if they could survive being a carpenter.

I woke them up early, around 7:00 a.m. for breakfast. We devoured our eggs, bacon and grits, hopped in the orange truck, and headed to the construction site. I could tell they didn't know what to expect. They were finally going to experience first hand, what their father did to put food on the table. I had to earn every dollar and I never felt guilty on paydays.

We arrived in Otay Mesa at 8:00 a.m. sharp. They were still a little tired and they weren't too excited when I pointed to the rooftop that we'd be working on from sunup to sundown. Our task was to nail down the plywood to the rafters and there wasn't any time for breaks. I gave them each a hammer, some nails and said, "Let's get to work."

After hours and hours of sweating, lifting and hammering, they were exhausted. It was around 4:30 p.m. and they were ready to go home. They were breathing heavy and dragging their feet as they headed towards the orange truck. I could tell by their long faces that my point got across. I didn't even have to ask. I got my answer. They didn't want to see another hammer and nail for a long, long time. They were thinking about college applications and nothing to do with a construction site. Even though I love the craftsmanship of carpentry and I would've been proud to pass along my hammer and tool belt, I was content with their decision. I wanted them to choose their own path. I also wanted to introduce them to hard work. Life is not a walk in the park and there's no such thing as a free lunch. In my experience, you have to work long hours of blood, sweat and tears to build a career and make a living.

What's funny is my lesson may have been too effective. Even now Harold, Marcus and Damon aren't too handy with the toolbox. I don't even think they could build a doghouse.

What's Wrong Is Wrong And What's Right Is Right

Entering the 1977 football season, head coach Vic Player had some tough decisions to make. He knew that if the Hornets were to have a legitimate shot at making it to the CIF championship, the offense would have to be able to put some points on the board. Coach Player was looking for some big-play potential and he saw Marcus as the spark that was needed. He decided to put Marcus at the quarterback position.

Marcus was already a tackling machine on the defensive side as a safety. By his senior year, Marcus was ready to roam around and be a dominating force like his favorite player, Detroit Lion defensive back, Lem Barney.

When Marcus got that news that he was going to play on both sides of the ball, he was not pleased. Playing quarterback was the last thing on his mind. He was thinking of getting interceptions instead of throwing them.

So what did he do?

Marcus decided in practice to fumble the snap on purpose, multiple times in protest to show that he was not the man for the job. Marcus figured that after his case of the butterfingers, he'd just get sent back to the defense and Coach Player would proceed with Plan B.

Well, Coach Player did have a Plan B. He did what any good coach would do. He kicked Marcus off the team. Instead of being sent back to his safety position, the best player on the team was sent home. A frustrated Marcus walked through the front door and told me what happened. I sat there and listened. After he was done, he paused and anxiously waited for my response. I casually said, "That's between you and Coach Player. If it takes you playing quarterback for the team to win, you need to play quarterback. Son, you gotta be a team player."

Marcus was shocked. He just assumed I was gonna offer him my unconditional support. He thought I was gonna go up to Lincoln and take care of business. But Marcus forgot, I was not only his father—I was a man of principle. Marcus was in the wrong. And what's wrong is wrong, and what's right is right. He was disrespecting the coaching staff and his teammates. *How could I support that?*

I could have easily crossed the line and let Coach Player have a piece of my mind. *"Who in the hell does Coach Player think he is kicking my son off the team?"* But that would have sent Marcus the wrong message. That would have shown Marcus that I endorsed his selfish behavior and that I believed that one player could be bigger than the team. We all know there's no "I" in team.

Marcus went back to Coach Player and rightfully apologized for his behavior. It's fair say, the rest is Lincoln Hornet history. The Hornets defeated the Kearny High Comets 34-6 in the CIF championship. Marcus scored all five of the team's touchdowns.

In hindsight, Coach Player was *more* than right. If Marcus didn't play quarterback, USC head coach John Robinson would've had no idea he could run with the football.

Nothing Ruins A Duck
But Its Bill

After Marcus's five-touchdown performance in the 1977 CIF victory over Kearny High School, we needed to purchase a second mailbox with all the recruiting letters that flooded our address.

During that time, a lot of coaches stopped by the house to offer Marcus a football scholarship. It was a learning experience for the whole family, and we appreciated every minute of it.

The coach's first job was to make a great first impression, especially with the player's parents. Personally, I could tell within seconds if a coach was nervous and if straight talk was in order. It's a tough gig for coaches. They have to watch what they say and how they say it. They must choose their words wisely. A coach can do a little quacking, say the wrong thing and the conversation can turn sour real quick.

When the Oklahoma Sooners came to the house, straight talk and a little extra was on the menu. The legendary head coach Barry Switzer, recruiting coordinator Jerry Pettibone and the electrifying NFL running back Joe Washington, wanted Marcus to play quarterback for the Sooners. Coach Switzer, born in Arkansas, was a country boy like myself, so we got along great. We were busy discussing life in Norman, and then suddenly he pauses and says, "Mrs. Allen, what's that good smell?" Of course, Gwendolyn with her New Orleans southern hospitality, quickly offered Coach Switzer and his colleagues a hot plate. Before you knew it, I was watching the head coach who perfected the wishbone offense, chow down on some of Gwendolyn's neck bones and collard greens. By his expression, I could tell he had a soft spot for her buttery cornbread.

The best connection I made was with Hudson Houck, the offensive line coach for the University of Southern California. He had been actively recruiting Marcus, even showing up to all of Marcus's basketball games. Hudson was honest and down-to-earth, qualities that a person from my part of town could embrace.

One night, after a game we learned that someone broke into Hudson's car and stole his sports coat. The family was shocked and a bit embarrassed, but that unsettling incident didn't diminish Hudson's Trojan spirit as he continued to make an appearance at the gym every Friday to watch Marcus's jump shot. After each game, Hudson and I would head to a local bar to shoot pool. We applied chalk to our pool sticks, worked on trick shots, talked about our childhoods and life in California. USC was never the main topic of discussion. The only thing I do remember telling him in regards to USC was that Marcus was gonna make his own decision. If Marcus wanted my two cents, I was more than glad to offer it.

When USC's head coach John Robinson visited the house, the straight talk continued. He was forward and to the point. He expressed his interest in Marcus as a defensive back and looked him in the eye, and stressed to him that he would have to compete for playing time. He didn't try to paint a perfect picture of the Coliseum crowd screaming his name. I liked his approach. It was not difficult to respect Coach Robinson.

On another note, a well-known coach from UCLA came by the house to recruit Marcus. He started off on the right foot when explaining the opportunities and advantages of attending his alma mater, and at first it was all smiles.

Then out of nowhere, I hear the words, "So send the boy to me and I'll raise him."

I immediately paused. On the outside, I kept a pleasant demeanor, but on the inside I was not too happy. Instantly, my two cents became $20. I don't know what type of man he thought he was dealing with, but I didn't find it funny. And if there was a punch line, I didn't bother to hear it. Maybe he felt too comfortable or he just didn't know that nothing ruins a duck but its bill. He might have been a UCLA Bruin, but he did too much quacking like an Oregon Duck. That type of language didn't fly in my house. Calling my son a "boy" and saying he'd raise him, every word I heard after that sounded like the excessive and annoying quacking of a duck. Just like a bad date, I started checking my watch.

Luckily, Marcus didn't have UCLA as his number #1 choice, but if he did, I would have given him my $20.

Don't Fall For The Okey-Doke

In 1981, when Marcus was a finalist for the Heisman Trophy, the family was invited to New York to attend the 47th Heisman ceremony at the Downtown Athletic Club. With excitement, we packed our jackets and scarves, and then boarded our flight, as we knew this was a once in a lifetime experience. Now at that time, I had never been to the city that never sleeps, but I heard too many stories about the tricks and trappings that the Big Apple could offer. New York is not for the naive. It's a fast-paced city where no one wants to miss an opportunity to make a buck. The challenge is knowing what opportunities to pursue and which ones to avoid. It's easy to get blinded by the bright lights. You could be looking directly at a scam, but trick yourself into thinking otherwise. When encountering opportunities with all the trappings, you must always think with a clear head, trust your intuition and use common sense. Too bad, some people I know weren't thinking at all. They messed around and fell for the okey-doke.

After being out and about for most of the day, the majority of the family was in our hotel room relaxing. Michael and my nephew Lonnie

109

wanted to continue sightseeing and pick up a few more souvenirs. They both had $40 each and they were looking to spend it. There were shops all around our hotel, so we felt comfortable letting them leave our sight. Before they could run to the door, I told them, "Beware of the Three-Card Monte guys, don't mess with them." They looked at me with a confirming nod then quickly took off.

Apparently, as they walked the streets they noticed a commotion and they just had to investigate. A voice yelled out, "Follow the lady, follow the lady...who can follow the lady?" What do you know, they saw a guy sliding three cards, face down in a circular motion on a cardboard box. The guy showed the crowd the target card, a Queen of Hearts, and then proceeded to quickly rearrange the cards so the crowd couldn't identify the target card. Once Michael and Lonnie saw how the game was played, they were lured by the chance of winning quick cash. They had no idea that when playing Three-Card Monte, they were actually playing against three hustlers. There's the dealer, who slides the cards around. There is the shill, a hustler disguised as an ordinary player, who happens to be on a winning streak. His role is to show the crowd that any average Joe can be a winner. Then there is the roper, a hustler in the crowd who ropes in the players, spreading false confidence in the air.

Michael got a strong whiff of that false confidence and felt it was a good time to try to double his money. They both confidently emerged through the money hungry crowd and stepped up to the dealer. They were shown the Queen of Hearts, and with a hint of arrogance, Michael made a $20 bet. He didn't believe in the old adage that "the hand is quicker than the eye." The dealer quickly rearranged the cards, toying with the Queen of Hearts with a "now you see it, now you don't" cleverness. Michael and Lonnie eyed the Queen, like bald eagles eyeing their prey. They watched closely, and when the cards stopped moving, they just knew the money was theirs to collect. Michael picked the middle card, and the dealer flipped it, revealing a King of Clubs. Michael was shocked, embarrassed and angered. He quickly placed another $20 bet. This time, the dealer rearranged the cards with even more speed, and then abruptly stopped. Michael picked the card to the left, a King of Spades and once again, he lost. Lonnie, being the loyal cousin, decided to try to recover Michael's $40. He dug into his pocket and placed a $20 bet. That didn't work. By that time, they were in too deep and within seconds, Lonnie's money was gone. In a New York minute, they lost a total of $80.

Up in the hotel, we were living it up, until we heard a knock at the door. We opened the door and saw Michael and Lonnie standing with their heads down, looking like sad puppies. Their hands were empty, their eyes were watery and they walked in at a snail's pace. Gwendolyn with concern, quickly asked, "What's wrong?" They stood quietly, exchanged a look at each other and then Michael explained to us what happened. Gwendolyn, Aunt Beverly, and Mama Alice were all falling for the sob story. Uncle Lonzo, Lonnie's father, began to chuckle and I immediately joined him. I don't know why they were caught up in the pity party, they were right there when I warned Michael and Lonnie about the Three-Card Monte guys. It's their own fault they fell for the okey-doke.

Even If The Fish Don't Bite, You Will Catch A Lesson In Patience

I never lost my passion for fishing, so I always knew the go-to spots throughout San Diego. The lakes in San Diego were always stocked with catfish, salmon, and fresh-water bass. My favorite spot was the San Diego River right behind Jack Murphy Stadium. Now it's called Qualcomm Stadium or "The Q". I still call it "The Murph." It was a hot spot for the colorful bluegill and the popular catfish.

Darius was 8 years old when I showed him a picture of the barbels on the face of the catfish that resembled "whiskers". He was eagerly ready to grab a fishing pole and experience his first day at the San Diego River. I was excited and hoping to gain a new fishing buddy. I also knew this would be a valuable lesson for Darius. I wanted to see if he had what it took to be a fisherman. I knew the whiskers intrigued him, but fishing isn't all about catching fish.

When we arrived at the river, we quickly settled at a nice, quiet spot with some shade. We found two big rocks that became our chairs, snapped open the tackle box and with optimism, tossed the wire basket into the water. When it came to putting the red worm on the fishing hook, Darius passed the test with flying colors. We both cast our fishing lines in the water, cracked open the Crush pineapple sodas, and kicked up our feet. Just in case our stomachs started growling, I had a bag of teriyaki beef jerky, a box of Red Vines and my favorite, black licorice. We had all the bases covered and it was now time to fish.

About two hours passed and we didn't receive a single bite. I could tell Darius was getting impatient and fidgety. He was probably itching for that darn Nintendo controller. Then he asked, "Why aren't the fish biting?"

I replied, "They bite when they're ready to bite. You must relax and be patient. You did your part. They will bite, they always do."

I guess those words didn't register. He was restless and I could see it in his face. I started to laugh as I continued to eat my black licorice and listen to the peaceful sounds of Mother Nature.

Moments later, I saw some activity far off in the lake that caught me off guard. Normally, I would've thought it was a fish swimming up to the surface to snatch a bug, but this splash was a little too big. That's when my relaxed smile disappeared as I turned to my right to witness Darius committing the biggest no-no in fishing. In the handbook of *What Not To Do While Fishing*, rule #13 clearly states,

"Thou shalt not throw rocks in the water." He quickly grew tired of waiting for a bite and decided to work on his pitching mechanics. I was not pleased, but then again I was far from surprised. I just didn't know he would decide to scare the fish away with his sidearm curveballs.

Darius watched too many infomercials on a magic lure called Gator Bait and thought the fish would be fighting over the worm on the hook. Just like most advertisements he'd seen on television, he expected instant results. He didn't grow up having adventures by the Red River and going through the growing pains of creating his own fishing pole. He grew up in the '80s with a microwave oven and a Texas Instruments calculator. He was accustomed to pushing a button and getting what he wanted. That's why I was happy to take him fishing, an activity that takes patience. To be a fisherman, you need self-control, restraint and poise. You also need these traits in life. I made sure Darius understood that some things take time.

I told him, "You're not always going to get what you want in life. If you do get what you want, you most likely won't get it when you want it." And that's a good thing. Like my mother said, "You gonna have good days and bad days. The key is to live with both." That's where patience comes in. Without patience, the ability to control your emotions is impossible. That's why *patience is a virtue*. Talk to anyone that you consider wise. They will tell you mastering patience is a must.

By the way, guess who walked away with a basket full of bluegill and catfish at the end of the day? There is no doubt *patience is a virtue*. Don't worry I shared some fish with Darius later that night for dinner.

A Father's Words

Raising A Daughter Is Like Raising Up A Mirror

I will be the first to say that being the only girl in a family of five boys is not easy. Any family with kids, regardless of birth order or gender, will face challenges. Kids love to battle for attention, wanting their voices heard loud and clear. They all want to add value and feel important. And ultimately, they all want to be loved. But all those challenges magnify, when you're the only girl in a family of boys.

As much as I would like to say you have to treat every kid equally, it's not the truth. Raising a daughter is not the same as raising a son. It's inherently different. I could not run away from that fact. There were times where I had to reconsider my tough love approach. With the boys, I made it a point to let them know I was their father and not their friend. My job was to teach them how to become men. I wasn't trying to be buddy-buddy. I wasn't a member of their crew. The goal was to instill discipline and responsibility. In time, I knew with love and respect, a strong friendship would develop. When it came to my only daughter

Michelle, I wanted to jump-start a friendship as early as she could say the word "Daddy". I needed our line of communication opened immediately. I couldn't afford to take any chances. There are just some things about being a girl that I will never understand—those aren't shoes that I can fill.

With a daughter, you become the student and she is the teacher. In my case, I was a full-time student and Gwendolyn was the principal. I could have been lazy and used my masculinity as an excuse to say, "Gwendolyn, you handle Michelle and I'll take care of the boys." But that's the easy way out. The goal is not to see how your daughter fits in your life, the goal is to play a role in hers. If you don't, she will spend her whole life trying to fill that void.

If your heart is in the right place, raising a daughter not only makes you a better father, it will force you to grow as a man. *If you think you have patience, wait until you raise a daughter. If you think you're a good listener, wait until you raise a daughter. If you think you know it all, wait until you raise a daughter.*

I wanted to raise a daughter that was strong and confident, one who felt beautiful inside and out. She had to know that her father would always be there for her. From the bottom of my heart, just like any active father, I wanted to be a part of her life as a mentor, provider and protector. I also wanted to be her friend—someone she could talk to about any and everything under the sun. To have that kind of father-daughter relationship, I knew I had to take an honest look at myself in the mirror. I had to look at my reflection to see who I was as a father and as a man.

As a result, I listened to the tone of my voice when I spoke, watched my words, and looked at my attitude. I searched deep inside myself and accepted the ongoing truth that I am a work in progress. So much work, that I often wondered if I was ever making progress creating that special father-daughter relationship. Looking at my only daughter Michelle was that constant reminder to look at the man in the mirror.

Even today at my age, Michelle can tell me, "Dad, that's not right." And as much as I might not show it, I think about her words. I may resort back to my comfy bed and flip on the television and watch a western, but then I start to think. I look in the mirror and I start to reflect.

Having someone hold up a mirror so you can see your reflection is not about exposing guilt or shame. It shouldn't be used as a tool to ridicule or to point out someone's flaws. The Lord knows we're all far from perfect. Fathers need to reflect on who we are. In order to become a better person, we all need to give the mirror an honest look. It's all about living up to your word.

As a father, I wanted love from all my kids, especially my daughter. Even if it took more overtime and I needed more assistance and guidance from Gwendolyn, I wanted to be in Michelle's life. I'm thankful that she is my mirror.

I Don't Know About The Birds And The Bees, But I Do Know That No One Wants To Be Lonely

I never had a formal sit-down with my kids about the "Birds and the Bees". I never understood the use of that story anyhow. Whenever my kids had a question, I was ready to give them a truthful answer. Whether they were ready for the truth or not. I told them what they needed to hear and not what they wanted to hear. The truth can open your eyes or it can make you want to cover them. When you're dealing with love and lust, most kids learn by trial and error, but there are just some errors you can't afford to make. For that reason, I never sugarcoated my words. Honesty is the best policy. I call it like I see it. Like the saying goes, "If it looks like a duck, walks like a duck, quacks like a duck, then it's a duck."

At my age, it's fair to say that I've been around the block. I've seen people fall in love, fall out of love, fall in lust, and some fall on their face. I've even seen Cupid draw back his arrow, take aim and miss his target. Love is not an easy thing—Cupid can attest to that.

Along with Cupid, I carried my own bow and arrow. You can't always wait for Cupid to take aim. I learned early that "closed mouths don't get fed" and I definitely wasn't shy when it came to the opposite sex. In my heyday, if you didn't approach and ask a girl out, then that meant you weren't going out. Your only company would be a lonely heart. It was that simple. The girl surely wasn't gonna ask. I had to step up to the plate and let my presence be known. That's how it was and that's how it will always be.

So here are a couple of things I've picked up during my courses on love and lust. There's no hand holding in this game. You either play the field or watch from the sidelines.

You Can Talk Yourself In, And You Can Talk Yourself Out

Men, it is no secret that women have a thing for words. This is why most fellas focus on "talking a good game". If your words are said with confidence, a little charisma and humor, you can make the type of impression that will get you in the door. Once you're in the door, make sure you do much more *listening* than talking. Become accustomed to taking a deep breath, closing your mouth, bracing yourself and trying your darndest to follow every word she says. Your story isn't the only one being told. You could sweet-talk, recite poetry and whisper sweet nothings all day and before you know it, that Casanova charm that you thought you had, will wear off and turn into an annoyance. Your good game is now a turnoff and now she doesn't want to hear anything you have to say.

You Are Not The Only Pebble On The Beach

Ladies, if your main goal in life is to make every head turn, before you know it, you're going to make every head turn away. Everything in life can't revolve around your outward beauty. You want to bring more to the table besides a makeup bag. Wanting to be attractive is never a bad thing, but being attractive on the inside is the beauty that never fades. As soon you think you're the hottest thing walking around, here comes another girl stealing your sunshine. *So what do you do then?* If you didn't know, men have been turning their heads since the beginning of time, so it's nothing to brag about. Instead of turning a head, what you really want to do is catch a guy's eye. And believe me, there is a difference. When you catch a guy's eye, he sees something other guys don't see and that's your inner beauty.

Let The Coach, Coach

Coaching from the stands was never my style. You could never catch me flipping through a playbook and calling plays from the bleachers. I never stood behind the backstop or walked up to the fence and advised my kids what pitch to watch out for. I've seen it happen so many times. Parents can't resist the urge to join the coaching staff. Even if you mean well, your actions will only undermine and show a lack of respect for the coach. You can approach the fence and tell your kid to watch out for that quick breaking curveball, not knowing the Third Base Coach is about to signal for a bunt. The majority of the time, you just end up interrupting the flow of the game and giving your kid more butterflies in their stomach.

Instead of coaching from the stands, I just quietly watched and let the game take care of itself. It is best to let kids deal with the challenges and results of the game on their own. It not only shows them that you trust their abilities; it allows them the opportunity to learn to trust themselves. *So why not let them get an early start on being accountable for their actions?*

Kids have to become familiar with success and failure on their own terms. There is absolutely nothing wrong with facing a little struggle. *You can't be there instructing them at every challenge they face. You can't be there to pick them up every time they fall.*

After the game, you'll have all the time in the world to offer your two cents. If you must and if you do, you better have some good advice to give. Just because you played the game, doesn't mean you know the game.

Don't Feel Guilty On Paydays

Every now and then, I may have to drop one of my favorite sayings on someone. It could be a young person who's just become a new employee or a grown-up looking for a fast buck. You might overhear me utter the words, "I know you feel guilty on paydays." It comes off as a joke, but we all know most jokes have a hint of truth. This saying is a subtle reminder of the benefits of hard work and earning every cent on your paycheck.

I've always valued hard work and that's because everything in my life that I value—took *hard work* to attain. Anything worth having—like a successful career, will not come easy. As a result, I developed a good work ethic and I learned that you never cheat your employer and yourself out of an honest day's work.

When you're on the clock, make sure you're focused on performing your duties. Keep your nose to the grindstone and complete every task with diligence. The goal is to acquire job experience and you have to understand that job experience is a portion of your compensation—that's the *portion* that will help you increase the dollar amount on your paycheck. It's no surprise that when someone is hiring, your job experience is their primary focus.

Keep in mind, your experience will also be a critical factor if you decide to become your own boss. It can kick-start your ambition to do your own thing and it can help you identify what business you should bring forth to the marketplace.

So whatever you do, don't be a clock-watcher and never be that employee that masters the art of dodging work—passing your responsibilities onto others and hiding out in the restroom. Unless you're having a case of the "rumbles in the jungle", there are only so many restroom breaks you can take.

When it comes to the workforce, the majority of employees fall into two categories: those that make the company money or those that lose it. That's what I call the employee bottom line. If you end up losing the company money, the next piece of paper you might receive is a pink slip. I suggest that before your first day of work, you make a commitment to go in every day with the mindset that you will earn your paycheck and then some. That way you will never feel guilty on paydays.

Another benefit to earning your keep and not cheating yourself out of job experience is that when you work hard for your money, you're more likely to keep it. There's the saying, "Easy come, easy go," and if you got your money easy, it normally leaves you easy.

Who's Helping You Steer Your Ship?

Over the years, I've been fortunate to call many people a friend. A title that shouldn't be used loosely or handed out frequently. If you're blessed enough to have a true friend, you'll realize how foolish it is to give that title to just anyone. It's important to know that everyone can't be your friend. You will meet some people you're better off keeping your distance from. On the other hand, you can't plan to have friends. Just make an effort to be sociable and friendly, and before you even use the word, they will just enter your life. They will come from different places, at unexpected times, and from all walks of life.

Throughout the years, I've always been aware of who came into my space. When a friendship developed, I was keen on judging the quality of that friendship. Things can be smooth sailing and then at a sudden turn, things can get rocky. That's why the key word in friendship is the word "ship". Do your friends keep your ship afloat or are they steering your ship into an iceberg? When a storm comes, do your friends stay aboard or do they abandon ship?

When it came to friendship, I asked myself

three questions. We all know a small leak can sink the "ship" in a friendship.

"Are you laughing more than crying?"

"Are you smiling more than frowning?"

"Are you looking towards the horizon or are you watching your back?"

These questions should be easy to answer. Keep it simple—have a good time, enjoy life, survive the storms and cross the ocean.

Learn To Be A Lone Wolf

There are no ifs, ands or buts around this—trouble happens. It happens to the best of us. Anyone can get caught in the wrong place, at the wrong time. Even the brightest of the bunch can find themselves on the wrong side of the tracks. Trouble comes in many different forms and for some, trouble is a way of life. The key is avoiding as much trouble as possible.

You don't have to live as long as I have to know that trouble is always lurking around the corner. I've had my run-ins with hustlers, fast-talkers and swindlers. I don't care to mention any names, but I've been pitched "opportunities" that sounded too good to be true. Those types of schemes where you're told that money grows on trees and you're guaranteed to see money falling from the sky. Yet, what you're really looking at is an orange jumpsuit and jail time. I've also witnessed my share of fistfights and scuffles. Some caused by a drunk patron and others by a no good heckler. I've seen a loud mouth try to act like a big man around his boys and write a check that his butt couldn't cash. Moments later, he's the first one laying flat on his back during the melee.

Truth be told, you can avoid a lot trouble in

life if you can spend time by yourself. Trouble likes to hang in a pack. Trouble always needs an accomplice. That's why through the years, I've grown to be a big proponent of being a lone wolf.

I'm not talking about being a lone wolf to escape your problems or run from the world. I'm not talking about being anti-social. I'm talking about choosing to be alone. Free to go and leave whenever you please. Knowing when to avoid the *riff-raff* and to make the decision to not follow the wolf pack. It's impossible to control the other wolves, but you can control yourself.

When kids succumb to peer pressure, it's not because they don't know right from wrong. It's usually because they find it difficult to stand-alone from the pack. To stand their ground and not roam wild. Along with being comfortable in your own skin, you have to be able to enjoy your own company. I never had an issue with being alone and enjoying my own thoughts. And I advised my kids, to be able to do the same.

If I was ever invited to anything that seemed a little sketchy or wasn't on the up-and-up, I had no problem telling that so-called friend, "No can do. I got plans. I'm hanging out with my other buddies."

"Who's your other buddies Red?"

"Me, myself and I."

Always Be Prepared To Have Something To Say

January 25, 2003, was a historic day for our family. On that Saturday afternoon, it was announced that Marcus was elected into the Pro Football Hall of Fame as a member of the Class of 2003. I can't describe the level of excitement that Gwendolyn and I shared. We were overwhelmed with joy. Our smiles lasted that entire day. As word spread to family and friends, phone calls came in by the hundreds. I saw Gwendolyn's face light up, and right then I knew Marcus was on the other end of the line. Understandably, Gwendolyn didn't want to get off the phone so I had to be patient. They were having a mother-son moment that I wouldn't dare interrupt. I waited my turn. Eventually, she passed me the phone.

> *"Congratulations Marcus."*
> *"Red, I want you to be my presenter."*
> *"What did you say?"*
> *"You heard me."*
> *"Why, thank you."*

As much as I would have loved to believe I was in contention for being a presenter, I never thought he would ask me. I've never been so shocked and honored at the same time. I just knew my late night speeches about the dirty dishes couldn't stand a chance against a fiery half-time speech by Tom Flores or Marty Schottenheimer. With an endless list of candidates, Marcus could have chosen anyone. Coaches and teammates who shared in his football journey, would have relished at this once-in-a-lifetime opportunity.

This indeed was going to be a special moment. I would become the third father in the history of the Pro Football Hall of Fame to present their son. In 1991, Herb Hannah became the first, presenting his son, offensive lineman John Hannah. Then in 2000, Roy Lott became the second, presenting his son, defensive back Ronnie Lott. Considering the number of members grew to 221, coming in third didn't sound bad at all.

I thought about a saying that Herbert Johnson always kept handy, *"Always be prepared to have something to say, for you'll never know when you're called on to speak."* Those words rang true. The enshrinement ceremony was in August, so I had plenty of time to write my speech, but my excitement took over and I immediately decided to put my thoughts on paper.

I was ready to toot the family horn. If there was ever an opportunity where I could address all the naysayers and critics that would be the perfect day. Don't think I wasn't aware of the snickers directed at my orange truck. Many from Southeast

San Diego and others from well-to-do communities throughout the county, wondered where we acquired our audacity to think big—to dream beyond 1003 Winston Drive. Marcus would be the first native San Diegan inducted into the Pro Football Hall of Fame. The legendary Ted Williams is in the National Baseball Hall of Fame and Bill Walton is in the Naismith Memorial Basketball Hall of Fame. I could flash my teeth and let out a big chuckle, solidifying that the Allen's got the last laugh. The stage would be set. The world would be listening. I grabbed a pen and started to write my speech. It didn't take long.

Once complete, I sat back, propped my feet up and started to read my speech. After thanking the Hall of Fame committee and welcoming back the old-timers on the 40th anniversary of the ceremony, I was embarrassed by what I read. All I did was brag and boast about Marcus's accomplishments. I realized that I was not prepared. I lost sight of what was important. Reciting a speech aimed towards the nonbelievers would be a waste of energy. *I didn't pay them any mind back then, so why would I pay them any mind now?*

I had an opportunity to speak the truth. Marcus didn't choose me so I could toot a horn or sing praises. Marcus was saying, "Thank you." My job as a father was to let Marcus know that I also wanted to say, "Thank you." Thank you for listening. That's the truth I lost sight of. I had a platform where I could speak for all fathers and it was my duty to let kids know that if they are willing to listen, we fathers just might have something to say —a few words of wisdom. Words that could be of some use.

I tossed that first draft to the side, letting months go by without making any revisions.

On August 3, 2003, at the Pro Football Hall of Fame in Canton, Ohio, I was prepared and I had something to say. I delivered my speech in the only way I knew how and it only came from one place— the heart.

I vividly remember arriving at the last paragraph. I took a deep breath and cleared my throat. The world needed to hear these words clearly:

Red

"Most of all, I cherish the time I spent with my son. Marcus, I pray that you will continue your faith in God, your love for family, your service to mankind. And, I stand here today as a proud father, and a good friend, to honor the man you are today. Ladies and gentleman, my son Marcus Allen."

Marcus approached the podium, we shook hands and he gave me a warm smile. That was one of my proudest moments as a father.

Be Strong In Heart And Strong In Mind

On October 31, 2012, Gwendolyn and I were aboard a United Airlines flight headed to Winnipeg, Canada for Damon's induction into the Canadian Football Hall of Fame. Seated quietly as we soared through the sky, I couldn't help but reminisce about the days sitting in the stands watching Damon play quarterback for the Lincoln Hornets. He led the Hornets to back-to-back CIF championships in 1979 and 1980 and on the pitcher's mound; he was a slender version of Bob Gibson.

I was on the plane thinking about how Winnipeg is a long way from Southeast San Diego. Heck, Winnipeg is a long way from Denison, Texas.

Damon played 23 years in the CFL. A career that took him to Edmonton, Ottawa, Hamilton, British Colombia and his last stop, Toronto. Damon was a barnstorming quarterback. He even played one year for the Memphis Mad Dogs, a CFL expansion team that folded in 1995.

We always tried our best to keep up with Damon's football journey. I remember buying a satellite dish and flipping through hundreds of fuzzy channels to find Damon's games.

Arriving safely at the Winnipeg International Airport, we picked up our luggage from baggage claim, and then we spotted our driver out front holding up a sign that read THE ALLENS.

That's when it hit me.

With Damon's induction, I would have two sons that will be members of a Pro Football Hall of Fame. Marcus in the NFL and Damon in the CFL. This is the first time that this has been achieved. Never would I have thought, an Allen bust would be on display in Canton, Ohio and another in Hamilton, Ontario.

It seems like yesterday, Gwendolyn and I were watching the kids water the dirt in the backyard to set up their first Mud Bowl. The fact that years later we were there when Marcus was awarded the MVP of Super Bowl XVIII, in 1983 and when Damon was the MVP of the 1987, 1993, and 2004 Grey Cups, is truly amazing. The Allen name has officially made an impact on the sports world across international borders. With pride, I can say, "The Allens were here."

There is no doubt that I'm a proud father—but keep in mind, I do not take any credit for my boys' performance on the field. You will never catch me talking about genes and genetics. I wouldn't dare claim that I taught Marcus the skills that allowed him to reverse his field and run 74 yards for a touchdown that would become a Super Bowl record. Nor can I say I had anything to do with

Damon audibling at the line of scrimmage, avoiding a pass rusher, and airing out a deep spiral for a Grey Cup touchdown.

To be honest, I enjoyed my seat in the stands. Football is a tough game. No matter if we're talking Pop Warner, high school, college, or the professional ranks. Once you get hit—I mean knocked on your butt—you either get back up or you decide to try another sport. Nothing is given in football. You have to be able to deliver and endure physical punishment. There is no way to escape that aspect of the game. If a man-to-man battle is not your thing, I suggest you pick up a baseball bat or even a golf club. There are no free throws, intentional walks, or free kicks in football. It takes heart and courage just to put on that helmet and snap on that chin strap.

Once you factor in the business side of professional football, the pressure to perform intensifies. There's also a game in the front office. One year, you're the focal point of the organization and the next year, the talk is about how you lost a step. You have to continually prove yourself day in and day out with your livelihood at stake. Not to mention, there is always someone waiting in the wings to take your position. To survive professional football and life in general, you have to be strong in heart and strong in mind.

As a father, I certainly treasure the success that Marcus and Damon have achieved. I enjoy the accolades, records and the Hall of Fame status, but I'm most proud of that fact that they battled and persevered against all odds.

I say with conviction that a father is instrumental in developing the mental toughness in a child. A father's job is to plant a mental seed of confidence that will eventually grow into the belief that any obstacle can be overcome. Physical talent is just for the sports field. Mental toughness is the part that transfers to any field in life. My sons just chose to play football.

Wherever their passion would take them, they had to be mentally ready to face an uphill battle. I wanted them prepared to climb a mountain. To make it to the top, you need the heart to compete; and you must believe you can outlast the competition.

So as their father, I challenged them. I held them accountable. I demanded their best with any endeavor they tackled. And as a result, Marcus and Damon were ready for that mountain.

When Marcus faced a contract dispute and years of reduced playing time from Raiders owner Al Davis, he kept his head up and didn't break. Although frustrated, his commitment to the game of football never wavered. He played for his teammates and continued to represent the best part of the Raider shield. I'm proud that his spirit was never broken. When the Kansas City Chiefs acquired him, he proved to his critics that his best days were ahead of him.

I'm equally proud that Damon stayed the course. For those that thought he was too fragile to play the quarterback position, he stood strong in the pocket for 23 years. When the sports media tried to define his talent, he kept the critics and opposing defenses on their toes, passing for 72,381 yards and rushing for 11,920 yards.

Marcus and Damon have given their heart and mind to the game of football and football has returned the favor. They are now moving on to new chapters in life. I'm at peace knowing that they are mentally prepared to climb the next mountain.

Marcus with his presenter, Red at the Pro Football
Hall of Fame enshrinement in
Canton, Ohio on August 3, 2003.

Gwendolyn, Damon and Red at the Bust Unveiling at the
McPhillips Station Casino in Winnipeg, Manitoba Canada on
November 1, 2012.

Watch What You Feed
Your Kids

After a charity golf tournament in Los Angeles, Gwendolyn and I were gathering our items and getting ready to head home. On our way out, a young lady approached us with a smile and some kind words. She knew our kids and was quite familiar with their stories. She told us she admired the job we did as parents. Gwendolyn and I were humbled. By no means do we put ourselves on a pedestal. We just worked as a team and tried our best to keep our family together.

Then she asked, "I'm curious, what did you feed your kids?"

I laughed and said, "The same thing you feed your kids…tough love, inspiration and motivation."

Are You Bragging Or Complaining?

This is a question that I've posed to many throughout my life. This simple question can quickly put life into perspective. Try it out. When you hear someone singing praises to the point where they only hear their own voice, just smile and politely ask them, "Are you bragging or complaining?"

Most will pause and think. Within that brief moment of silence, a thing called perspective will enter the conversation.

If you're bragging, you might want to tone it down a bit. No one really wants to hear you toot your own horn when everyone is concerned about the music of their own band.

And if you're complaining, I sure hope there are solutions at the end of your gripes. No one wants to hear about your problems when there are more than enough to go around.

That's why when I get asked, "How's life treating you Red?"

I always reply, "I can't complain and if I did, would you listen?"

That normally gets answered with a chuckle.

At the end of the day, I can't complain even

if I tried. I've been blessed and sitting back, counting my blessings is one of my favorite pastimes. God is good.

Keep Your Promises

I often think about the promise that I made to myself at my father's funeral. The vow that if I ever got married and became a father, I was going to be the best father that I could be. I had no idea at the time what it took to be a father, let alone a husband.

I was just listening to my heart.

I will leave it up to my wife and kids to determine my performance on the job. There is no manuscript on how to be the ideal father for your family. During all my years as a father, I've focused on being the constant provider, but I've come to realize that my family has provided me with the most valuable lesson. I've learned that being a father and adhering to the responsibilities is more than worth it. Accepting the challenge and not just the title of father has enriched my life beyond anything that I could imagine.

I kept my promise and in return, my family has kept me surrounded with the best gifts in life. I've been given unconditional love, uncontrollable laughter, and endless joy—so much that I don't recall the heartache and pain of life. Now that's what I call living!

They say there's nothing new under the sun

and the more things change the more they stay the same. And that's the truth. We all need love from our family.

I'm truly blessed to have Gwendolyn, Harold, Marcus, Damon, Michael, Michelle and Darius in my life. Although I may be stubborn at times and rigid in my point of view, I appreciate my family's willingness to let me do my job. I'm privileged to be the father of the family. At my young age of 79, I'm still keeping my promise.

The Allen family at the 50th Wedding Anniversary of
Red and Gwendolyn.
(From left to right) Darius, Michelle, Marcus, Michael,
Harold Jr., Damon. (Seated) Gwendolyn and Red.

www.ingramcontent.com/pod-product-compliance
Lightning Source LLC
Chambersburg PA
CBHW040750150426
42813CB00067B/3035/J